THE MATE
OF THE LILY

NOTES FROM HARRY MUSGRAVE'S LOG BOOK

W. H. G. KINGSTON

1st WORLD
LIBRARY
Literary Society

The Mate of the Lily

W. H. G. Kingston

© 1st World Library, 2007
PO Box 2211
Fairfield, IA 52556
www.1stworldlibrary.com
First Edition

LCCN: 2007930919

Softcover ISBN: 978-1-4218-4872-3
Hardcover ISBN: 978-1-4218-4775-7
eBook ISBN: 978-1-4218-4969-0

Purchase *"The Mate of the Lily"*
as a traditional bound book at:
www.1stWorldLibrary.com/purchase.asp?ISBN=978-1-4218-4872-3

1st World Library is a literary, educational organization
dedicated to:

- Creating a free internet library of downloadable ebooks

- Hosting writing competitions and offering book publishing
scholarships.

Interested in more 1st World Library books? contact:
literacy@1stworldlibrary.com
Check us out at: www.1stworldlibrary.com

1st World Library Literary Society

Giving Back to the World

"If you want to work on the core problem, it's early school literacy."

- James Barksdale, former CEO of Netscape

"No skill is more crucial to the future of a child, or to a democratic and prosperous society, than literacy."

- Los Angeles Times

"Literacy... means far more than learning how to read and write... The aim is to transmit... knowledge and promote social participation."

- UNESCO

"Literacy is not a luxury, it is a right and a responsibility. If our world is to meet the challenges of the twenty-first century we must harness the energy and creativity of all our citizens."

- President Bill Clinton

"Parents should be encouraged to read to their children, and teachers should be equipped with all available techniques for teaching literacy, so the varying needs and capacities of individual kids can be taken into account."

- Hugh Mackay

CHAPTER ONE

Jack Radburn, mate of the "Lily," was as prime a seaman as ever broke biscuit. Brave, generous, and true, so said all the crew, as did also Captain Haiselden, with whom he had sailed since he had first been to sea. Yet so modest and gentle was he on shore that, in spite of his broad shoulders and sun-burnt brow, landsmen were apt to declare that "butter wouldn't melt in his mouth."

A finer brig than the "Lily" never sailed from the port of London. Well built and well found—many a successful voyage had she made to far distant seas. Jack Radburn might have got command of a larger craft, but Captain Haiselden, who had nursed him through a fever caught on the coast of Africa, and whose life on another occasion he had saved, thus closely cementing their friendship, begged him to remain with him for yet another voyage, likely to be the most adventurous they had ever yet undertaken.

Jack Radburn, who was my uncle, stayed when on shore— not often many weeks together—with his sister, Mrs Musgrave, my mother.

Though he was my uncle, I have spoken of him as Jack Radburn, mate of the "Lily," as did everybody else; indeed, he was, I may say, as well known as the captain himself. My mother, who was the daughter of a clergyman long since dead, had not many acquaintances. She had been left by my grandfather with little or nothing to depend upon, when her brother introduced to her my father, then first mate of the ship to which he belonged.

Her greatest friend was Grace Bingley, who lived with her mother, wife of a ship-master, a few doors off from us.

Uncle Jack had consequently seen much of Grace Bingley, and had given her the whole of his warm honest heart, nor was it surprising that he had received hers in return, and pretty tightly he held it too. Even my mother acknowledged that she was worthy of him, for a sweeter or more right-minded girl was not, far or near, to be found.

Some four years before the time of which I am now speaking, my father sailed in command of a fine ship, the "Amphion," for the Eastern seas. The time we had expected him to return had long passed away. My mother did not, however, give up all expectation of seeing him, but day after day and week after week we looked for him in vain. The owners at last wrote word that they feared the ship had been lost in a typhoon, but yet it was possible that she might have been cast away on some uninhabited island from whence the crew could not effect their escape. My mother therefore still hoped on and endeavoured to eke out her means so as to retain her house that my father might find a home should he return.

I was setting off with Uncle Jack for the "Lily," which was undergoing a thorough repair, and he seldom failed to pay her one or two visits in the day to see how things were going on, when two seamen came rolling up the street towards us in sailor fashion, and looking, it seemed to me, as if they had been drinking, though they may not have been exactly drunk.

W. H. G. Kingston

As they approached one nudged the other, and, looking at Uncle Jack, exchanged a few words.

They would have passed us, when he, having noticed this, hailed them—

"What cheer, my hearties, have we ever sailed together?"

"Can't say exactly, sir, for we've knocked about at sea so long that it's hard to mind all the officers we've served under. But now I looks at you, sir, I think you used to come aboard the 'Amphion' before she left Old England. We heard say you were the captain's brother."

"The 'Amphion!'" exclaimed Uncle Jack, eagerly, looking hard at the men. "Can you give me any news of her?"

"Aye, sir, but it's bad news."

"Out with it, whatever it is," exclaimed Uncle Jack, fixing his eyes on the man, to judge whether he spoke the truth.

"It's a matter of over four years gone by when we sailed for the Eastern seas. We had been knocking about in them parts for some months, when we were caught in a regular hurricane, which carried away our topmasts and mainyard, and did other damage. At the same time we sprang a leak, and had to keep the pumps going without a moment's rest. When night came on, and a terrible dark night it was, sir, matters grew worse and worse, not a hope but that the ship would go down, though we well-nigh worked our arms off to keep her afloat. Howsomedever before long, she struck on a reef, though she hadn't been thrashing away on it three minutes when she drove off, and the water came rushing in like a mill stream. 'Out boats,' was the cry. Bill here and I, with three others, got into the jolly-boat, but before another soul could spring aboard her she drifted away from the ship. We felt about, and found a lugsail and an oar. To go back was more than we could do, and it's our belief that scarcely had we left her than the ship went down. As our only chance of keeping the boat afloat was to run before the sea, we stepped the mast and set the lug close reefed, hoping to come upon some land or other. When morning broke no land was in sight. We thought we saw what looked like it far away on the starboard quarter, but we could only go where the wind drove us. Three days we scudded on without a drop of water or bit of food to put into our mouths. I speaks the truth, Bill, don't I?"

"Ay, ay!" said Bill, looking as if he did not even like to think of that time; "you does, mate."

"Go on," said Uncle Jack.

"Well, first one went mad and jumped overboard, then another died, then another, and I thought that Bill would die too, when down came a shower, and with the help of our sail we filled an empty breaker which we had in the boat. Then we knocked down a bird which came near us, and that gave us a little more strength. Then three flying-fish came aboard, which kept us for three days more, and after that we caught a small shark, but the water came to an end, and we were both so well-nigh done for that neither Bill nor I could hold an oar to steer by, nor knew where we were going—I speaks the truth, don't I, Bill?"

"I suppose you does, but I don't mind much what happened then. I was too bad," said Bill.

"Well, as I was a-saying, I thought it was all over with us, when a ship hove in sight and took us aboard. She was a foreign craft, and not a word of what her people said could we make out, any more than they could understand us. We were not over well treated, so we ran from her the first place we touched at; and after knocking about for a long spell in them South Sea islands among the savages, in one craft or another, we got home at last. What I've told you is the blessed truth; ain't it, Bill?"

Bill grunted his assent to this assertion; he evidently was not a man of words.

My uncle cross-questioned the men, but could get nothing more out of either of them. Whether or not he was perfectly satisfied I could not tell. Still it seemed too probable that the "Amphion," with my father and all hands, was lost.

Having lodged the seamen so as to find them again, my uncle returned with me to my mother. She was prepared for the information he had to give her. She had for some time been persuaded of what everybody else believed, that my father was lost, and she now knew herself to be a widow. It was a severe shock to her notwithstanding. She looked at me and my five brothers and sisters, all younger than I was.

"What shall I do with these fatherless children?" she asked, while her eyes filled with tears, thinking more of us than of herself; "my means are almost exhausted, for my dear husband saved but little, and I shall not have the wherewithall to pay the rent of this house, much less their food and clothing."

"God has promised to provide for the fatherless and widows," answered Uncle Jack; "while I have a shilling in my pocket it shall be yours, Mary. Harry, too, is able to support himself. We'll take him aboard the 'Lily,' and soon make a prime seaman of him."

My mother looked at me, grieving at the thought that I must so soon be taken from her. Then other thoughts came into her mind.

"But you, my dear Jack, require all the means you possess for yourself. Grace has promised to become yours whenever you desire it."

"I know that," answered Uncle Jack. "I prize her love, but we are both young and can wait, and true as mine is for her it must not overcome my duty to you and yours. Captain Haiselden talks of some day going to live on shore, when he will give up charge of the 'Lily' to me, or I may obtain a larger craft and shall make enough for Grace, and you, and myself, I hope. At all events, my dear sister, you and the children must not starve, and we shall have Harry here making his fortune. So cheer up, Mary, and trust in God."

"I do, Jack, I do," she answered, taking his hands, while the tears still flowed down her pale cheeks. "Harry will do his duty, I know, and some day be able to help me, and I must try to do what I can for myself, though I fear it will be but little."

"You have friends who will be glad to lend you a helping hand," said Uncle Jack, who judged of others by himself. "We may have, I trust, a successful voyage, and all will go well, Mary."

Much more he said to the same effect. My mother appeared comforted, at all events she grew calm, and as Captain Haiselden consented to take me on board as an apprentice, she set herself busily to work to prepare my outfit, while my sister Mary, who was next to me, and my two younger brothers were sent to school, and Grace Bingley came in every day to assist her in her task.

How industriously Grace sat working away with her needle, every now and then jumping up to prevent Frank or Sally from getting into mischief! Some of the larger garments were certainly not for me. My mother had promised to overhaul Uncle Jack's wardrobe and supply what was wanting, according to a list he gave her. I should like to describe Grace as she sat in the bay window opposite my mother with the work-table near them, but it will suffice to say that she was young, fair, and pretty, with eyes that seemed to have borrowed their colour from the sky. My mother had assumed the widow's cap, and might from her clear complexion, and her brown hair braided across her brow, have been taken for Grace's elder sister. Though the heart of Grace must have been sad enough I suspect, she talked cheerfully, endeavouring to distract my mother's mind from the thoughts of the past as well as the approaching parting from me. I came in occasionally and found the two sitting as I have described, but I was generally on board the brig with Uncle Jack, assisting in fitting her out, and thus got initiated into many of my duties before I ever went to sea. The captain often came on board during the evening to see how we were getting on, but during the day he was mostly engaged in looking out for freight in addition to the cargo he intended to ship on his own account. He was just the man the crew were willing to serve under, his countenance exhibiting sense and determination, and a kindly spirit beaming from his eyes; his hair grizzled rather by weather than by years; his figure, of moderate height, broad and well knit, betokening strength and activity.

We were to sail for Singapore, after which we were to proceed eastward to trade with the various islands in that direction.

We expected to have the "Lily" ready for sea in about a week, when just before this time Captain Bingley, who had been long absent in command of the ship "Iris" of some four hundred tons, returned home. I was at my mother's one evening when Uncle Jack, with Grace Bingley, came in. She looked, I thought, somewhat out of spirits. My mother thought so too, and asked her the cause. She hesitated for a moment as if to master her feelings, and then said—

"It is, I have no doubt, for the best, and father wishes it. Mother and I are to accompany him on his next voyage round Cape Horn and up the western coast of America, then across the Pacific to Java, and so round the world. I cannot refuse to go, and of course we should both like to see strange lands, as well as being with father, but I had hoped to be able to remain with you, Mary, and you know how happy I should have been in doing so."

My poor mother looked much distressed. "Of course, if your father wishes you to go you have no choice, but I shall miss you greatly." She could scarcely restrain her tears as she spoke.

Uncle Jack became very grave as he heard what Grace said.

"You sail round the world! Has your father positively determined on this?" he asked.

I guessed his thoughts; he was ready enough to encounter all the risks and perils of the sea himself, but he was very unwilling that Grace should be exposed to them. What if the ship should be wrecked! What if sickness should break out on board, or a mutiny occur, or should she be captured by an enemy! He dreaded dangers for Grace which he did not take into a moment's consideration in regard to himself, but he strove not to allow her to perceive his anxiety.

"Father is not a person, as you well know, to be turned from

W. H. G. Kingston

his purpose," she answered, trying to smile. "Mother has promised to go, and I cannot let her go without me. She or father might fall ill, for he is not so strong as he was, and I ought to be ready to nurse them, and I hope, my dear Jack, that we shall be back as soon as you are, though my chief anxiety is leaving Mary; and Harry also away. Perhaps, too, we may meet; my father doesn't know exactly where we shall go after we leave the China seas; it must depend upon the freight obtained."

"It is a wide region, and I was hoping that I could picture you when I was away, safe at home," answered Uncle Jack, but he refrained from saying more. He was unwilling to create any anxiety in Grace's mind. He certainly, however, looked more distressed than any of the party.

After this Grace could be less at our house than usual, as she had to help her mother in preparing for their voyage. The "Iris," she told us, was to be got ready for sea with all despatch. Uncle Jack and I one evening went on board to have a look at the ship that, as he observed, he might at least know what sort of a craft Grace was sailing in. The cabins were comfortably fitted up and well suited for the accommodation of the captain's wife and daughter, as well as for a few other passengers. I asked him what he thought of the ship.

"She's a fine enough vessel, but I can judge better of her if she were loaded, and I should like to know what sort of a crew she has," he answered. "Captain Bingley is a good seaman, and I respect him as Grace's father; but he wants to make money, and he may be tempted to overload his ship, or visit dangerous places to obtain freight."

I did not see the parting between Uncle Jack and Grace, as I went on board the "Lily" the night before we sailed. I had already wished good-bye to my dear mother and all the young ones, and as she had to look after them, she could not come to see us off. I know very well what she must have felt, and I heartily wished, when the moment came for leaving, that I could have remained to comfort and protect her. My going away must have brought back to her recollection with painful vividness the time when my kind father last sailed I suspect she thought that she might never see me again; still she knew that I must work for my livelihood, as I did myself, and I was going to begin the profession I had chosen, and for which I had long had a desire. For dangers and hardships I was ready, fully persuaded that, though I might encounter, I should get through them.

We were at sea at last, running down channel with a fair wind. Uncle Jack had had no difficulty in obtaining a good crew, for when he could find them, he picked up old shipmates, who were always glad to sail with him. He had promised Timothy Howlett and Bill Trinder to look them up, and they, having spent the last shilling in their pockets, were glad to ship on board, he hoping that they having been before in those seas might be useful. James Ling was second mate and Sam Crowfoot boatswain, making up the complement of our officers, besides which there was our supercargo, Edward Blyth, a young but very intelligent man, who had already made a voyage to the Eastern seas, understood Dutch as well as the Malay languages, and was thus able to act as interpreter at many of the places where we were going. He was well informed on many subjects also, and possessed a good knowledge of natural history. I must not forget "Little Jem," the smallest boy on board. Instead of being knocked about and bullied, he was somewhat of a favourite among the men, with whom, however, he was pretty free and easy in his way of talking; but they liked him all the better for that. To the officers he was always respectful, well-mannered, and, being very intelligent and active, was consequently a favourite with them.

We had on board four carronades and a long gun, as where we were going it was necessary to have the means of defence, but they were stowed below during the first part of the voyage. We had also a supply of cutlasses, pistols, and boarding pikes for all hands, which ornamented the fore bulk head of the main cabin, though occasionally taken down to be cleaned and polished, so that they might be of use when wanted.

Uncle Jack took great pains to teach me navigation, and, as I had learnt mathematics at school, I was soon able to take a good observation with my sextant and to work out the calculations correctly. A knowledge of seamanship I found was not to be obtained so rapidly, though Crowfoot, the boatswain, was always ready to give me instruction and express his opinion how a vessel ought to be handled under all possible circumstances, but a large amount of presence of mind, and what may be called invention, has to be exercised on numerous occasions, for which no rules can be laid down.

"Now, Harry, you see wits is what a sailor wants. You've got learning, and with learning you can pick up navigation pretty smartly. I haven't got the learning, and so I can't get a mate's certificate; but I've got the wits and have been many a long year at sea, and so I am fit for a boatswain, and can take charge of a watch with any man," he remarked.

The wind favouring us after we left the chops of the channel, we ran into the north-east trades, which took us to within two or three degrees of the equator; and after that we had the calms and heavy rains which are invariably met with, and were sometimes wet to the skin, at others roasted in the hot sun. No one suffered, however, and after getting out of them, we picked up a fine south-east trade wind. This carried us down to twenty-six degrees south. The meridian of the Cape was passed about the fiftieth day after leaving the Lizard. We ran down our easting on parallel forty south. The brig was going about eight knots before the wind, when one morning there was a cry of "Man overboard!"

Uncle Jack, who had been below, sprang up the companion-ladder, and, looking over the side, saw that it was little Jem, who had fallen from the fore yardarm. Ordering all hands to brace up the yards and the man at the wheel to put down the helm, while he threw off his jacket, he leaped overboard and struck out for the boy.

"Heave a grating here!" he shouted. "Harry, don't come," and I, who was on the point of following, did as he directed.

The captain was on deck a moment afterwards and made ready to lower the lee quarter boat. Every one on board, as may be supposed, was busy pulling and hauling and bracing up the yards and backing the main topsail, so that there was no time to see what had become of the first mate and boy, but the captain had his eye upon them. It was sharp work, for we knew the lives of our fellow-creatures depended upon our exertions. I wished that I had possessed the strength of two men. As soon as the brig was hove to, I took one glance to windward. I thought I saw Uncle Jack and the boy, but I also saw what filled me with alarm, a huge albatross flying above, apparently about to swoop down upon them. It was but a glance, for I sprang over to the other side to jump into the boat, eager to be among those going to save them. The second mate was already in the boat, three other hands following. As soon as we got under the stern of the brig, we saw the captain standing aft, pointing in the direction we were to steer. The second mate, I thought, appeared very cool.

W. H. G. Kingston

"Give way, lads," he shouted. "We shall be up to them before that bird strikes either of them on the head, for it seems that is what he is trying to do."

A long rolling sea was running, and only when we were at the top of a wave were those ahead of us visible to the mate, who stood up every now and then the better to watch them.

"There's that bird making another swoop!" he exclaimed, and soon afterwards he cried out, "He has risen again. Give way, lads! He may not have struck both."

I did give way as may be supposed. If one had been struck, might it not have been Uncle Jack!

"He has hold of the grating at last!" cried the mate. "I see him waving his hand. There comes the bird again!"

Once more my heart sank within me. I could not turn round to look, or I might have missed my stroke. The boat seemed to be making but fearfully slow progress as I watched the brig rising to the seas, and as she pitched into them, throwing the spray over her bows. There stood the captain pointing with his hand, as if to encourage us to persevere. On and on we pulled, I expecting every moment to hear the mate exclaim that the albatross had made a fatal swoop. At last I heard a voice, though a very weak one, cry, "Take the boy in first."

I knew it was that of Uncle Jack; I saw him lift little Jem up while he held on to the gunwale. The two men in the bow then hauled him in, and next the grating on which he had supported himself.

Uncle Jack sank down utterly exhausted. We passed the boy aft. He seemed to be dead. We then dragged the first mate into the stern-sheets, but could not attend to him, for we were compelled to keep our oars going to get the boat round as soon as possible. Uncle Jack lay without moving. I saw that one of his shoes was off. He presently came to. His first thought was for the boy, whose hands and chest he began to chafe as well as his weakness would allow.

The second mate, I thought, might have spared a hand to help him, but he looked on, it seemed to me, with indifference, jealous that the first mate should have behaved so gallantly, or—although I tried to put the thought from me—angry that he had escaped. We pulled away until rounding the stern of the brig, we got alongside, when a cheer burst from the crew as they saw that we had the first mate and little Jem safe. Eager hands stood by to lift them or board, for even Uncle Jack was still too weak to help himself. While the boat was being hoisted up the captain directed Mr Blyth and me to carry the boy into his own cabin, he and two of the men following with the first mate, who was placed in his own berth. We, in the meantime, had got the boy's clothes off him and had wrapped him up in a dry blanket, while we kept chafing his chest, arms, and feet until he breathed freely. He soon returned to consciousness, and looking about him was much surprised to find where he was.

"Where's Mr Radburn? Oh, sir, have you got him safe?" was his first question.

He is all right, my lad.

"It's that bird, sir; it's that bird, sir! Oh, save me from it!" he continued crying out.

"The bird won't hurt you, and Mr Radburn is safe in his cabin, I hope," answered Mr Blyth, in a kind voice.

W. H. G. Kingston

As soon as I could I went to see how the first mate was getting on. He had swallowed a cup of hot tea, for we were just going to breakfast, and this had greatly restored him; and though the captain had advised him to be still, he was putting on his dry clothes, and in a short time joined us at table.

Uncle Jack said that he had felt the tips of the bird's wing pass over his head each time that it swooped down, but that he had taken off his shoe and attempted to defend himself, until the bird had seized upon it and carried it off. "It will find the shoe a tough morsel to digest," he added, laughing; "but truly I have reason to thank God that it did not strike either little Jem or me with its sharp beak, and I was so exhausted that if the boat hadn't come up when she did, I should have been unable to keep him longer at bay."

Either Mr Blyth or I stayed by "Little Jem" all day, the captain and first mate every now and then looking in. By night he was well enough to be removed to his own berth forward, where the men promised to look after him.

The captain and Mr Blyth complimented the first mate on his gallant conduct, but he seemed to think he had done nothing out of the way.

"There is one thing a man should consider before he jumps overboard, and that is, whether there is too much sea on to allow of a boat being lowered, for if there is he will not only lose his own life, but cause the loss of others," observed the captain. "It is a hard matter, however, to lay down a rule. Still it is very certain that we should do our best to save the lives of our fellow-creatures."

We once sighted an island, which I believe was one of the Crozet group. In rather over three months we entered the Straits of Sunda, when, as we were approaching shores the inhabitants of which were addicted to piracy, we got up our guns from the hold and mounted them, and overhauled our firearms. Before long we had a good chance of requiring them, for when running through the Straits of Banca, between that island and Sumatra—while nearly becalmed—we made out three large prahus full of people, pulling towards us. Whether their intentions were friendly or the reverse we could not ascertain, but we certainly did not like their looks; a breeze, however, sprang up and we stood on our course. Soon afterwards we came in sight of the fine town of Singapore, founded in 1819 by Sir Stamford Raffles, who made it a free port. At that period a wretched village stood on its site, the neighbouring harbour being the rendezvous only of a few trading prahus. It is now a magnificent city, and upwards of a thousand square-rigged vessels anchor annually in the roads. On the hills beyond it can be seen the residences of the merchants, surrounded by plantations of spice-trees, while excellent roads with bridges over the streams run in all directions.

Besides English churches and chapels, there are Chinese Joss houses, Hindoo temples, and Mohammedan mosques, while large numbers of Chinese and Malay cottages form the suburbs. The Chinese are here seen in considerable numbers, being the most industrious part of the population, and include many wealthy merchants. There are Klings from Western India; Arabs, chiefly shop-keepers; Parsee merchants; Bengalese, mostly grooms and washmen; Japanese sailors, many of whom are also domestic servants; Portuguese clerks, and traders from Celebes, Boli, and other islands of the vast archipelago.

Having discharged part of our cargo, we took on board such articles as we heard were in demand among the natives with whom we hoped to open up a trade. In the interval Mr Blyth proposed that he and I should make a trip into the interior.

We could not, however, go far, for the island is only about twenty-seven miles in length and eleven in breadth. We were particularly warned not to venture into the forest, as we should run a great risk of being carried off by tigers, large numbers of which infest the jungles, and, it is said, kill a Chinaman a day, they being the chief workers in the plantations. The captain gave me leave to accompany the supercargo, and we hired two small Timor ponies for our excursion. We had not got far when we met a party of men carrying between them the skin of a large tiger, propped up on a sort of platform formed of bamboos, looking very fierce, with its mouth open and tail on end. They were on their way to the government office to receive the reward given for every animal killed, just as payment was made in former years in England for the head of each wolf put out of existence. The animal had been caught in a pit covered over with sticks and leaves, the usual mode in which they are trapped. We kept a sharp look-out, with our pistols ready to shoot a tiger should one attack us. We heard several roars, and a huge beast crossed the road in front of us. After this we did not feel altogether comfortable, expecting every moment that it would spring out from the jungle and carry off one or both of us.

We returned to the city, however, without an actual encounter. I cannot stop further to describe this interesting place. In a few days we sailed for George Town on the eastern side of the island of Penang, the seat of Government of the British possessions in the Straits of Malacca, Penang is larger than Singapore, a considerable portion being rocky, and those most industrious of mortals, the Chinese, form the chief part of the population. After discharging the cargo we had brought from England for this place, we again sailed, steering through the straits of Singapore for the eastward.

CHAPTER TWO

We were bound for Kuching, the capital town of the province of Sarawak in Borneo, where Mr Brooke, who went out in 1839 in his yacht the "Royalist," had, by his judgment and intrepidity, established a thriving community, of which he had been appointed the chief or rajah. The captain and supercargo had mapped out our future course. This was to be along the north coast of Borneo, through the Sooloo archipelago, across the sea of Celebes to the coast of Papua, and thence through the Banda sea to Timor, whence we were to return home along the southern coast of Java. It took two days to get up to Kuching, the capital of the province of Sarawak, after we had entered the mouth of the river on the banks of which it stands. On either side were hills covered with jungle, with here and there clearings where the peaceably-disposed natives had established themselves.

Mr Blyth and I had an opportunity, in company with a gentleman who was making a shooting expedition, of taking a trip into the interior. I wish that I could describe the magnificent vegetation, the gigantic trees, and the curious animals we saw. One of the most curious was the mias. What is a mias? will be asked. It is the native name of the far-famed ourang-outang, the principal wild inhabitants of this region. We were proceeding through the forest, with our guns, when one of our Dyak companions came running up to tell us that he had seen a mias, and that if we made haste we might be in time to shoot it.

We hurried on, the Dyak leading the way, until we entered a thick jungle. He pointed to a tree far above our heads. Upon looking up we saw a great hairy body and a huge black face gazing down upon us, as if wondering what strange creatures we could be. Mr Blyth and our friend fired; whether they had hit the mias we could not tell, but it began to move away among the higher branches at a rapid rate. Led by the Dyak we followed, when again we caught sight of it on the branch of a tree, where it remained for a minute or more. By this time we were joined by several other Dyaks, whose shouts appeared to frighten the ourang-outang, which tried to get along the edge of the forest by some lower trees, keeping, however, beyond the reach of our rifles. The Dyaks, flourishing their weapons, rushed on ahead of us hoping to have the honour of killing the monster. We had lost sight of them for a few seconds, when we heard fearful shrieks and shouts, and running forward, we saw that the mias had either voluntarily descended the tree, or had fallen to the ground, and had rushed at one of the natives, who, unable to escape, was standing with his spear ready to defend himself. We were afraid in attempting to kill the mias that we might shoot the native, when, just as the creature was about to seize the man with its mouth and formidable claws, our friend fired and the animal fell, shot through the heart.

On measuring the mias, from the top of its head to its heel, we found that it was four feet two inches long, while its outstretched arms measured seven feet three inches across. Its head and body were of the size of a man's, the legs being very short in proportion. This mias was of the larger species, many being under four feet high, and some of the females not more than three feet six inches.

We saw a frog, with large web feet and inflated body, fly from the top of a tall tree. It was about four inches long, the back and limbs of a shining black hue, with yellow beneath. Our friend had promised us a rich treat at supper, and he produced a fruit which he told us was the Durian. It was of the size of a large cocoa-nut, the husk of a green colour, and covered all over with short stout spines. It grows on a lofty tree, somewhat resembling the elm. It falls immediately it is ripe; but the outer rind is so tough that it is never broken by the fall. There are marks which show where it may be divided into five portions; these are of a satin whiteness, and each one is filled with an oval mass of cream-coloured pulp, in which are two or three seeds about the size of chestnuts. This pulp is the eatable part. Its consistency is that of a rich custard. As to describing its taste, that is more than I can do. It is not acid, nor is it sweet, nor juicy, but yet, as we ate it, we agreed that none of these qualities were wanting, and that it was the most delicious fruit we had ever met with. The Mangosteen, which comes to perfection in Borneo, is another splendid fruit of a sub-acid flavour, better known than the Durian. But I must not stop to give long descriptions either of the animals or fruits we met with. Blyth and I had to return, as we could not long be absent from the brig.

Often had the now smiling plantations through which we passed been plundered by blood-thirsty pirates, and the heads of their inhabitants carried off. A visitor on board gave us dreadful accounts of the atrocities committed by the pirates in the seas through which we were to sail.

"We will show them that they had better not attack us," observed Captain Haiselden, pointing to our guns. "The 'Lily' is a match for all their fleets put together."

"Not if the 'Lily' is caught at anchor or in a calm; you may then find that they are too much for her," was the answer.

W. H. G. Kingston

"These prahus often carry sixty men or more, with guns and small arms, and you would find it no easy matter, were you to be attacked, to beat them off."

"They'll not stop us; but we will keep a bright look-out for them," answered Captain Haiselden.

We had a fine breeze as we ran along the coast of Borneo, and although we saw in the distance not a few long suspicious-looking prahus, we sailed too fast for them to overtake us. We saw one of these crafts lately captured, which had been brought to Kuching. She was about ninety feet in length, and of proportionate beam. In the bow she carried a long twelve-pounder gun, and six swivels on each broadside, besides which she had thirty or forty rifles or muskets on board, and other small arms, swords, pistols, and pikes. She pulled eighty oars in two tiers, and had had a crew of a hundred men. Over the rowers, extending the whole length of the vessel, was a light flat roof composed of fine strips of bamboo covered with matting, which, notwith-standing its lightness, was very strong. This deck served as a platform, on which the fighting men stand to fire their muskets or hurl their spears, while the rowers below them sit cross-legged on a shelf projecting outwards from the bends of the vessel.

The Dyak piratical vessels are called "Bang Kongs." Although they are a hundred feet in length by ten in beam, they draw but little water, and are both light and faster than the Malay prahus. They have long overhanging stems and sterns, are propelled by eighty paddles, and are as swift as any craft afloat. Some mount a few small swivels, and each carries a certain number of Malays armed with muskets, besides which they have their regular crew of Dyaks, whose weapons are spears. From drawing so little water they are much dreaded, as they can run up the shallowest river, when their savage crews, landing, commit most horrible atrocities on the inhabitants living near the banks.

We had left Sarawak about three days, when it fell almost calm; still the vessel was making some way through the water. I was stationed forward to keep a look-out. As I turned my eyes around the horizon ahead I fancied that I could distinguish what appeared just like a small number of black dots rising above it. Before I sang out, however, asking the boatswain, who had come on the forecastle to take my place, I ran aloft, with a spy-glass slung to my back, to satisfy myself whether I was right or not. Reaching the fore-topmast cross-trees, I took a steady look in the direction I had seen the dots I was convinced that they were prahus, though whether large or small I could not be certain, pulling towards the coast of Borneo. I counted six altogether. On my return I went aft to report what I had seen to the captain.

"We will keep away a little, and pass astern of them. They may possibly not have seen us, or if they have, they'll think it prudent not to come nearer."

The first mate on hearing my report also went aloft, and on his return corroborated it. I confess that I felt somewhat uneasy at the sight of these vessels. They might be peaceable traders, but they might be pirates, who, should they find us becalmed, might try to obtain a rich booty such as our vessel would afford them.

I was surprised that my uncle and the captain took the matter so coolly. I watched the strangers until they were no longer to be seen from the deck. After some time we again hauled up and stood on our course to the eastward. Later in the day, on going aloft, I again caught sight of the prahus, as I believed them to be, but as they were very low in the water, they were scarcely visible to any but a sharp pair of eyes,

W. H. G. Kingston

such as I possessed.

In the afternoon I was taking a turn on deck with Mr Blyth, the captain and first mate being below, and the third mate in charge of the brig, when I observed a small cloud coming up on the port bow.

"There's wind in that cloud, I'm sure," I said to my companion. "I'll point it out to the mate, for he doesn't seem to see it." I did so.

"That's all you know about the matter, youngster," he answered in a scornful tone.

"We shall be taken aback if we don't shorten sail, and I don't know what will happen," I remarked to Blyth, when I rejoined him. "I have a good mind to run down and tell the first mate."

Scarcely had I said this, and was about to spring down the companion-hatch, when Mr Ling sang out—

"Ready, about ship!"

The helm was put down, the yards were being braced round, and the brig's head brought to the wind, when, as I looked up, I saw every sail aback. At that moment I heard the voice of the captain, who had just come on deck, shouting, "All hands shorten sail and save ship," but the order was given too late. The squall I had seen coming up just then struck her, and in one moment, with a fearful crash, the main-mast fell. I should have been crushed had I not by tumbling head first down the hatchway avoided it; the next instant the foremast followed, and the bob-stays giving way, dragged the bowsprit on board. The moment the crash was heard the first mate sprang up the companion-ladder shooting me with his head on deck again. I looked round expecting to see many of the crew killed. My eye first fell on Mr Blyth, who was holding on by a stanchion, and apparently uninjured. The second mate, too, excepting a blow on the shoulder, had escaped, while of the crew, though they looked very much astonished, not a man was seriously hurt. Several of them, indeed, who had been below, had only rushed up on hearing the crash of the falling masts. They were gazing with open eyes on the utterly dismantled state of the brig, lately so taunt and trim, waiting for the captain's orders what to do. But what had become of him? He was nowhere to be seen. At first I feared that he had been knocked overboard, but as I looked about I caught sight of a man's legs sticking out from under a mass of sails and rigging. Knowing that it must be the captain, I ran to drag him out, calling on Blyth to assist me.

We soon got him free, but he did not move; we feared that he was dead. At Blyth's suggestion, with the help of two of the men, we carried him below and placed him on his bed.

Greatly to our relief he in a short time began to show signs of life.

"He will soon come round," said Blyth; "I will watch him, so do you go on deck, Harry, where I am sure you will be wanted, and tell the first mate how he is getting on."

I hurried up, and reported the captain's state to my uncle.

"Thank heaven!" he exclaimed; "I had no wish to take his place, but I must attend to the work before us—we have plenty of it."

He then turned round to the bewildered crew—

W. H. G. Kingston

"We must first haul in all the gear trailing overboard, my lads, and then get up jury-masts," he shouted out, hurrying along the deck to examine the state of things forward.

Having got the spars and rigging on board, we commenced unbending the sails and unreefing and coiling away the ropes. As we got the yards free we stowed them amidships, that we might use those of them which were most suitable for jury-masts. The wind had in the meantime been increasing, and the sea was getting up. All we could do was to keep the vessel before it, while we laboured hard to rig a jury-mast forward that we might, as soon as possible, get sail on the brig to steady her. She was now rolling fearfully, and it was with difficulty even that we could keep our feet. I looked out more than once in the direction where I had seen the prahus, fearing that should they discover our present defenceless condition they might attack us, for although we might fight our guns it would be at a great disadvantage.

The gale blew harder and harder. I had not heard for what port the first mate intended to steer, though I of course knew that he would endeavour to make one as soon as possible, either Sarawak or Singapore; but as the gale was at present blowing us away from both of them until we could get up jury-masts and haul our wind it would be impossible to reach either the one or the other. There were numerous dangers in the way which would at all events have to be encountered.

We were moving sluggishly on amid the fast rising seas, when I saw an object in the water, still at a considerable distance ahead. Now it appeared on the summit of a sea, now it sank into a hollow. It looked so much like the wreck of a vessel that I reported it to the first mate.

"Maybe some unfortunate craft capsized by the squall, a fate which might have been ours had not the masts given way," he observed. "We'll endeavour to keep close to her in case any of the crew may have escaped and be clinging to the wreck."

As we got nearer I jumped up on the forecastle, when I saw that the object was a vessel of some sort, but not an European craft. She was a prahu, probably one of the fleet we had before seen. In a short time I perceived that there was some one on board clinging to the stern, which was the highest part out of water.

I at once told the first mate. He and the second mate held a short consultation as to the best means of rescuing the person—pirate as he might be, we could not leave him to perish.

Some spars had been lashed to the stump of the foremast on which a royal had been set, and this enabled us to have the brig somewhat under command. Ropes were got ready to heave to the man. The boatswain, who took the helm, steered the vessel so as to pass close to the wreck without the danger of running her down. Immediately the brig's side touched her a rope was hove to the man, who was standing up ready to catch it.

"Haul away!" he shouted, as he clutched it firmly, and several willing hands being ready to haul him in. The next instant he was on board the brig, while the wreck, bounding off from us, dropped aft, about, it seemed, to plunge beneath the foaming seas.

"Why, my lad, who are you?" asked the first mate, who had assisted him on board.

"I am an Englishman," was the answer of the stranger, but he in vain tried to say more.

W. H. G. Kingston

"Though you are pretty well sun-burnt, you have an Englishman's face sure enough, though you seem to have lost the use of your tongue."

"Long, long time no talk English," replied the man, who seemed to understand pretty clearly what was said to him. We had too much to do, however, to spend time in asking him questions.

Before night we had some spars lashed to the stump of the main-mast, which enabled us to set a little after sail and bring the vessel to.

It was of the greatest importance not to run further eastward. Happily the wind shifted, and getting the vessel's head round we steered for Singapore. The gale, too, began to abate, and the sea to go down, so that we were able to carry on our work with less difficulty than had before been the case. The dangers in our course were numerous, but we hoped, by constant vigilance, to avoid them.

CHAPTER THREE

We had an anxious time of it as we made our way back to Singapore, between islands innumerable and coral reefs below water, on which it was often with difficulty we avoided running. The first mate was seldom off the deck, and Crowfoot, the boatswain, showed that he did not boast without justice of his seamanship.

It is on such occasions that a sailor has an opportunity of proving what he is made of. The wind continued fair and the weather fine, or our difficulties would have been greatly increased. The less I say of the second mate the better. Uncle Jack did not trust him, and while it was his watch on deck constantly sent me up, or made an excuse for running up himself to see how matters were going on. He insisted also on taking his share in attending on our poor captain, who remained in his berth unable to move, and, as we feared, in a very precarious state. Blyth and I assisted in nursing him, but the second mate, through whose carelessness the brig had been dismasted and the captain injured, refused to take the slightest trouble to help us—indeed, he kept out of the cabin altogether. The young man we had rescued from the Malay prahu gradually regained his recollection of English, but from the first he showed an unwillingness to talk about himself, and I observed that he kept aloof as much as possible from the crew. When I asked his name he said it

W. H. G. Kingston

was Ned Light, that he had been wrecked somewhere to the eastward, and, narrowly escaping with his life, had been taken prisoner by the pirates, who had kept him ever since in bondage. He appeared to be more ready to talk to little Jem than to any one else, and the two were constantly together. When I tried to find out from the boy what account Ned gave of himself, Jem was remarkably reticent. At length, however, one day he said, "He seems to be afraid of some of the men, sir. He thinks that they intend to do him harm, but I cannot find out why he has got that idea into his head. I told him that he might trust you and the first mate, but he only answers, 'Better not talk.'"

All had gone well in consequence of the constant watchfulness and untiring efforts of the first mate, when, as we were within about four days' sail of our destination, while rigging out a boom on which to set a square sail, one of our best hands, Dick Mason, fell overboard. The brig was running about four knots through the water, and as Mason could swim well, no one felt much apprehension about his safety. The sails were instantly clewed up, and the only boat which had escaped injury was at once lowered. Ned and I, with Crowfoot, the boatswain, and two other hands jumped into her and pulled away towards our shipmate, who was striking out boldly to meet us. Before the boat was lowered, however, the brig had run some distance, and we had a considerable way to go. Just as I was going down the side I saw a black fin rising above the surface, passing close under the stern. The boatswain I knew had seen it too, for he urged us to use our utmost exertions to reach Mason, and sang out to him to keep splashing about with all his might. We did our best, making the oars bend again. We were within half a cable's length of the poor fellow, when a fearful shriek reached our ears. I instinctively turned round just in time to see his head disappear beneath the bright surface. There was a ripple where he went down, and as we got up to the spot and looked into the depths of the ocean we could see a struggling human form surrounded by a ruddy tinge, and the glittering white of the shark's lower jaws. Ned, who was in the bows, plunged down his boat-hook, but Mason's hands were already far below the point he could reach. The next instant the shark had disappeared with its prey.

All hope of recovering even the body of our poor shipmate was gone, and we returned with sad hearts on board.

"He is a great loss to us," remarked the boatswain. "He was one of the men I could always trust, and that's more than I can say of some of the rest."

"But Tim Howlett and Trinder are smart hands, surely?" I observed.

"They may be, but I don't like their goings on. If others trust them, it's more than I do."

"I am sorry to hear you say that of the men," I remarked. "I fancied that they were about the best men we have on board."

"You haven't seen as much of them as I have, or you wouldn't say that of them," replied the boatswain.

"I'll give a hint to the first mate of what you think," I said.

"No use in doing that. He generally has his weather eye open, but he's too generous to believe evil of a man unless he has strong proof. You must leave him to find the matter out for himself."

At last we sighted the island of Singapore. Instead, however, of bringing up before the town we made a signal for three

W. H. G. Kingston

boats, which towed us into the new harbour. There we came to an anchor close to the shore, and were able to refit much more rapidly than we could have done in any other place. Our crew generally laboured away from sunrise to sunset without complaining. But Howlett and Trinder grumbled at the additional work they had to perform. The second mate seemed always out of humour, and went about his duty in a listless fashion, frequently abusing the men without any cause for so doing. The captain, who was getting better, would not allow himself to be taken on shore to the hospital, asserting that he was much more comfortable on board with Mr Radburn, Blyth, and me to look after him, than he should be there. We, however, persuaded him to let us send for a doctor, who came, and, greatly to our relief, assured us that he was going on favourably, although it might be a long time before he would be able to attend to his duty on deck. The first mate had asked Ned if he would enter in place of Mason, but he did not—as I thought he would have been glad to do—accept the offer.

I spoke to him, advising him to remain, assuring him that he would be well treated.

"The first mate and boatswain are kind to me, but I think, sir, I had better ship on board another vessel homeward-bound," he replied.

I asked him, however, to remain a day or two, which he agreed to do. Next morning, when the hands were mustered for work, Howlett and Trinder were not to be found. I was sent on shore to look for them, it being supposed that they were not far off, but after a long search I had to return on board and say that I could not find them. There was a creek a little way off lined with mangrove bushes. The captain therefore directed Mr Blyth and me to take one of the boats and pull up it with four hands, all of us well-armed, thinking

that the deserters might have concealed themselves somewhere on its banks, hoping to get an opportunity of making
their way over to Singapore.

We had got a short distance up the creek when I saw a vast
number of dark objects hanging to the bows of the mangrove
trees.

"Are those things fruit, or are they the nests of birds?" I
asked, pointing them out to Mr Blyth.

"Neither one nor the other," he answered: "those are bats, or,
as they here are called, flying foxes. As we return they will
be on the move, and you will then see what they are like."

"I will take the present opportunity," I answered, and
steering the boat closer in to the shore I observed that there
were thousands and tens of thousands of the creatures
hanging by their claws to the boughs in a most curious
manner as thick as a swarm of bees. With a boat-hook we
pulled off two or three, which falling inboard were picked
up. They showed, however, no fear, nor did they make any
attempt to escape, but licked our hands and appeared
perfectly at ease. The head was like that of a miniature fox,
and the skin was beautifully soft. Blyth told me that they live
upon fruit, large quantities of which they consume. On
reaching the head of the creek we found a hut, in or about
which it was supposed that the runaways might have
concealed themselves, but we could discover no traces of
them, and consequently judged that it would be useless to
search further in that direction.

The dusk of evening had come over as we pulled down the
creek, and the bats had begun to stir. Presently the whole air
was filled with them as they took their flight towards the
plantations where they were about to forage. They looked,

W. H. G. Kingston

with their wings stretched out, of wonderfully large size, so as literally to darken the sky.

The next day passed and still we could hear nothing of the two men. The captain on this sent Blyth and me over to Singapore, where we found that they had entered on board a homeward-bound ship and had sailed. With the assistance of the agent we succeeded in replacing them by two other Englishmen, and we also engaged four Lascars, fine active-looking fellows, who were likely to prove of much use, as they could endure the heat of the sun better than could our own men.

The captain inquired whether the man we had picked up had entered.

"He has been working very steadily," answered the first mate, "but Harry shall ask him if he intends to remain."

When the men knocked off work I went forward to speak to him.

"Well, Ned, what have you determined on?" I asked; "the captain wishes to know whether you will enter."

"I will very gladly do so, Mr Harry," he answered. "I like you and the first officer, and as I have no friends at home who care for me, I am in no hurry to get back to old England."

"Why were you unwilling to enter before?" I inquired.

"Well, sir, I don't mind telling you now. It was on account of those two fellows, Howlett and Trinder. I have served with them before, and us I know a thing or two about them, and that they are mutinous, ill-disposed rascals, I was afraid that they would find me out, and some dark night heave me overboard, or knock me on the head."

"On board what ship did you serve with them?" I asked.

"On board the 'Amphion,'" he answered. "They and several others of the crew, tarred with the same brush, stole a boat and deserted from her, leaving us so short-handed that, one of the officers and two other hands being washed overboard, when the ship caught in a typhoon we were unable to manage her, and she drove on a reef and was lost, we who remained scarcely escaping with our lives."

"The 'Amphion!'" I exclaimed, much astonished. "Why, that was my father's ship! Did you say the captain escaped?"

"Yes; all of us, except one poor fellow, got safely on shore, but it was a wild place, and we found ourselves among savages, who threatened to take our lives, but they did not, though they ill-treated us, and made us work for them."

"Do you think the captain is still alive? Can you pilot us to the place?" I inquired eagerly.

"All I can say is that the captain was well in health, though sadly cast down, when I last saw him," answered Ned. "As to finding the spot where we were wrecked, that is what I fear I cannot do, for I don't know even the name of the country; and as I am ignorant of navigation, and was soon afterwards carried away by the Malay pirates, who took me about with them from place to place, I have lost all reckoning, though I calculate that it was somewhere away to the eastward. I think, however, that I should know the country if I saw it again, though these islands are so much like one another that I could not be certain; but do you say, sir, that you are Captain Musgrave's son? I have only heard you called Mr

Harry, and I did not know it before, or I should have spoken to you."

"Yes, Captain Musgrave, who commanded the 'Amphion,' was my father, and we have long given him up for lost," I replied. "Do you think that he remained at the place where the ship was wrecked, or was he carried off by the pirates?"

"He was not carried off by those who took us, for he and the first mate and two seamen had gone up the country, and so escaped. Three others were taken with me, but what became of them I do not know, may be they were drowned or krissed by the Malays, as I never saw them again; indeed, it is a wonder that I am alive, seeing what I have gone through. The fellows who first got hold of me did not keep me long, but sold me to another gang. They and I were afterwards wrecked, and when we were trying to make our escape on board some canoes we had built, we were overtaken by another fleet of pirates, who killed most of my companions. They spared my life, but sold me after some time to the people to whom the prahu belonged, from the wreck of which you picked me up."

"You must come aft and narrate what you have told me to the first mate," I said.

I ran down to tell the captain and first mate, who directed me to bring Ned below, that they might hear his story. Having cross-questioned him far more than I had done, they were perfectly satisfied that he had spoken the truth, though they found it impossible to make out where the 'Amphion' had been wrecked. They put a chart before him, but he was utterly unable to guess where the wreck had occurred, or even to point out Singapore, where we then were. Thus we were left in doubt whether the 'Amphion' had been lost on the coast of Borneo or on that of Celebes or Gillolo, or even as far east as New Guinea.

Ned's account made my uncle and me more eager than ever to continue the voyage. The captain fully entered into our feelings, but at the same time he felt that it was his duty to attend to the interests of the owners, and to visit only the places where trade could be carried on. The Dutch, who hold possession of Java and many of the Spice Islands to the eastward, throw so many difficulties in the way of commerce for the sake of keeping it in their own hands, that the captain had been directed not to visit any of their ports if he could avoid doing so. Our object therefore was to trade chiefly with the natives, from whom we were more likely to learn something about the wreck of the "Amphion" than from the Dutch, for it was considered that if they had had any communication with the survivors of her crew, means would have been found to send home an account of the occurrence. Now, as I have said, nothing had been heard of the "Amphion" when we left England, nearly four years after the time it was supposed she had been lost, beyond the statement made by the two men who said they had escaped from her. Ned's account showed that the owners were right in their conjectures as to the possibility of her having been cast on some desert shore, instead of having gone down, as was more generally believed, in a typhoon. By working night and day, we at length got the "Lily" *ataunto*, and we were thankful when being towed cut of harbour we found ourselves with a fair wind standing to the eastward. We had the same dangers of coral reefs, sand banks, and low islands to encounter as before, but we were in a better condition now to avoid them.

Having passed the island of Labuan—since taken possession of by the English—on the north-west of Borneo, we stood along the coast until we rounded the northern end of that large island. To give some idea of the size of Borneo, I may say that the whole of England, Ireland, and Scotland, with the Orkney and Shetland Islands, would fit inside it, leaving a very wide margin all round in addition. We were talking about the inhabitants, when Uncle Jack observed—

"With the exception of Sarawak in the west, the whole of this magnificent country is in a state of barbarism. The few Malay settlements along the coast are but very slightly removed from the same condition. It is said that the chief delight of the Dyak tribes, who inhabit the interior as well as the larger part of the coast and the banks of the rivers, is to attack their neighbours for the sake of obtaining heads, and that no lover can present himself before his intended bride until he offers her one of those gory trophies as a proof of his prowess. The greater the number of heads he can present, the more willing the damsel becomes to receive his advances. Notwithstanding such a peculiar custom, the Dyaks possess many excellent qualities. They are said to be truthful and honest, generally intelligent, kind tempered and mild, and tolerably industrious; superior indeed in many respects to the Malays and Chinese, who cheat and plunder them.

"While we are opening up Africa, it seems to me that we should make an effort to civilise and carry the blessings of Christianity to the numberless inhabitants of Borneo beyond the province of Sarawak."

We passed through the Straits of Balabac, between Borneo and the long island of Palawan into the Sooloo Sea, said to be infested by pirates, who have little difficulty in escaping pursuit among the numerous islands to the south, forming the Looloo Archipelago. To the east of us were the Philippine islands, owned and misgoverned by the Spaniards.

We, however, kept along the coast of Borneo, and though pirates might have swarmed in its bays and rivers, we were fortunate in not falling in with any. We met, however, several traders, Chinese as well as Malay, from whom we made inquiries through Ned respecting the wreck of an English vessel in those seas. Blyth also endeavoured to obtain information as to where the articles we wished to procure were most likely to be obtained. The captain of one of the Malay vessels came on board us to do some trading on his own account. As he seemed inclined to be communicative, we put several questions to him through Ned, who was evidently highly interested in the replies he received.

To our questions as to what the Malay said, Ned replied, "He tells me, sir, that he has heard of several white men being at a village on the banks of a large river some way up from the coast. As far as I can make out, they have been there a long time, and the natives won't let them get away. The people he speaks of may be Captain Musgrave and some of my old shipmates; but yet it does not seem to me from the sort of country he describes that it can be near the place where the 'Amphion' was lost."

We told Ned to inquire if one of the men belonging to the prahu would be willing to pilot us up the river, promising him a handsome reward if he would do so, and undertaking to set him on shore at any place he might name which we could reach. For this purpose the first mate, Blyth, and I, taking Ned, went with the Malay captain on board his vessel. Summoning his crew, he explained the object of our visit and the offer which had been made. After a long palaver a man stepped out and expressed his readiness to accompany us. The Malay captain, after a short talk with the man, introduced him to us, saying that his name was Kalong, that he was well acquainted with the coast and an experienced sailor, as indeed are most of the Malays of the archipelago. This matter, with which all parties were pleased, being settled, we returned to the "Lily," and sail was made for the

W. H. G. Kingston

part of the coast where Kalong informed us we should find the mouth of the river. We hove to soon after sunset that we might not pass the spot during the night.

When Kalong came on deck at daybreak, we once more stood in for the coast. The wind, however, was light, so that we made but little progress. He pointed to the southward, indicating that we must steer in that direction. At length, to our great joy, we saw what was evidently the mouth of a large river, fringed thickly with mangrove trees.

Ned shook his head. "That's not where the 'Amphion' was cast away," he remarked, as we stood towards it. "Still it may be, notwithstanding, that our friends are up there. Kalong says that there is water enough for the brig all the way up to the village, but he thinks it would be wiser to anchor just within the mouth and let only the boats go up, as the wind might fail us and we might have a hard job to get out again. As it is a long pull he also advises that the boats should leave the brig in the evening, so as to get to the place the next day."

This advice exactly agreed with what the first mate thought best, and Captain Haiselden, whom he consulted, was of the same opinion. We accordingly, the wind favouring us, stood on and brought up just inside the mouth, which formed a beautiful harbour. We lost no time in getting ready for our expedition. Two boats were lowered, each pulling four oars, the crews consisting of four Englishmen and four Lascars, besides Kalong and Ned, the first mate and I going in one and Mr Blyth and the boatswain in the other. We were all well-armed, and had provisions for a couple of days. We also carried a number of articles for trading with the natives, whom we hoped, from Kalong's account, to find friendly.

We had thus left but a small number of men on board, but as

the brig was in a safe place, the captain, trusting to Kalong's report, considered that there was no risk of her being attacked by pirates. I heard him tell the first mate, however, when we went into his cabin to wish him good-bye, that he should have a sharp look-out kept, the guns loaded, and all hands armed in case of accident; and, he added, "Remember, Radburn, that you are to run no unnecessary risk; don't trust the natives too much, and keep your party well together if you land, so as to be able to get back to the boats. Kalong may be a very honest fellow, but it is as well not to rely too much on him. If you hear of any Englishmen being in the village or neighbourhood, get Kalong to open up a communication with them, and send a written note to ask who they are."

"Aye, aye, sir!" answered Uncle Jack; "you may depend upon my discretion."

I naturally felt very eager, for I had persuaded myself that we should certainly find my father, notwithstanding Ned's doubts. I do not think my uncle was quite so sanguine, still he was very willing to undertake the expedition. We had on board a small light canoe, which we had brought from Singapore, large enough to carry two or three people, but easily paddled by one. At the last moment it was determined to carry this canoe with us, as she could tow astern, and might be of great use in sending ahead to act as a scout.

As soon as everything was ready we shoved off, our ship-mates remaining on board, giving us three hearty cheers as we pulled away. We found that the river made several bends, so that in a short time we were out of sight of the brig.

As we passed close, sometimes to one bank, sometimes to the other, we could hear the cooing of pigeons, the shrill call of peahens, and the notes of many song birds; above which rose the chattering of troops of monkeys, while parrots and other gaily-coloured birds flew from bough to bough. The monkeys occasionally showed themselves, leaping along the branches, often running out to those above our heads and uttering hoarse cries, as if ordering us away from their domains, grinning fiercely at us, hooting and chattering, and shaking the boughs in their indignation.

We had got up some distance, and calculated that it would be dark in the course of a short time, when, having entered another reach, we saw before us on the right hand shore an opening in which were several huts, of a construction common in that country, being erected on tall posts with a ladder leading to them.

Kalong said that he was not aware of any village being there, and that it had probably not long been established. As we could see only three huts, and as there were not likely to be many inhabitants, he and Ned offered to go on shore and obtain information, while we remained in the boats with our arms ready for use, should the natives show any signs of hostility. Uncle Jack, however, directed us to keep our weapons concealed, while we had, besides the English ensign, a white flag flying in the bows of our boat.

Blyth, on hearing of the plan, wished to land, and my uncle, after a little hesitation, gave me leave to accompany him, provided we kept behind Kalong and Ned until they had ascertained the character of the people. We accordingly at once pulled in for the bank. Kalong and Ned sprang on shore, Blyth and I fallowing. We had pistols in our belts, and each wore a sword; but, as the Malays all go armed, such weapons were not likely to make them suppose that we were otherwise than peaceably disposed.

We had not proceeded far, when several Dyaks, who had

apparently been watching us from their elevated dwellings, came down the ladders which led from them to the ground, and made friendly gestures, inviting us to advance. The men wore waist cloths of blue cotton which hung down behind, and were bordered with blue, white, and red. Their heads were bound with handkerchiefs of the same colours. They wore earrings of brass, and heavy necklaces of black and white beads. On their arms were a number of rings of white shells or brass, their long shining black hair hanging over their shoulders, and to their waists, secured by a belt, was a pouch with materials for "betel" chewing. In the belt was stuck a long slender knife, and most of the men held in their hands a knife-headed spear.

The women, who were better clothed than the men, wore coils of rattan to which their petticoats were fastened round their waists, besides which their arms and legs were ornamented with rings of brass wire, and their heads by hats of curious shape, adorned with beads. They had generally a pleasant expression of countenance, and appeared ready to afford us a friendly welcome.

Kalong and Ned at once entered into conversation with them, as they seemed perfectly to understand each other. No information, however, could be obtained about the white men of whom we had heard. Without hesitation they came down to the boats, bringing some mats and other articles which we purchased at a very moderate rate. They had also with them some curious monkeys with enormous noses, faces of a brick-dust colour, and about as ugly specimens of the monkey tribe as I ever saw.

Their bodies were about three feet in length covered with thick fur, of a bright chestnut-red. I am almost afraid to say how long their noses were, but they stuck out with the nostrils at the tips and had certainly a most curious appearance. The arms and legs had somewhat of a whitish tinge, and the hands were grey rather than black. Ned told us that they were very active, and when at liberty could be seen leaping from branch to branch, generally in large troops, holloaing loudly as they go along. Blyth purchased a couple, as they were very tame and seemed well-mannered. He hoped to be able to keep them alive if he could obtain suitable food.

After a short and satisfactory intercourse with our native friends, we shoved off and proceeded up the river. The tide, however, soon turned, and Uncle Jack, considering that it would be useless to attempt pulling against it, brought up for the night a short distance from the left bank, but sufficiently far off not to run the risk of being surprised by hostile natives.

As we had a long pull before us, the first mate arranged that all hands should lie down except two in each boat to keep watch, that we might be the better able to work the next day. Supper, however, was first served out, for we had hitherto not had time to eat anything. It was arranged that Ned and I should have the first watch in our boat, and as soon as supper was over, the rest of the party stowed themselves away as best they could on or under the thwarts. The boats lay in the shadow cast by the tall trees on the bank nearest to us, from which strange sounds ever and anon came off, produced either by wild beasts or insects, not sufficiently loud to drown the ripple of the water as it flowed rapidly by. The bright stars shone down from a cloudless sky on the surface of the stream, flickering and dancing in the eddies caused by the current.

I found great difficulty in keeping awake, though, of course, I did my best to prevent my eyelids from closing by constantly shifting my position and looking round in every direction, not that I apprehended danger, but from knowing that it was my duty to be prepared for any contingency.

I had been on watch for an hour or more, when Ned, who was seated on a thwart, stepped aft. "Hist, Mr Harry," he said, in a low whisper, "do you hear the sound of voices coming down the river?"

I fancied that I did.

"Just listen."

I listened, and after some time could distinctly hear some strange sounds, though I was not certain that they were those of human voices. I awoke the first mate, who also heard them.

"If you like, sir, Kalong and I will pull up in the canoe and try and find out where they come from," whispered Ned; "it may be that the natives are only holding one of their harvest feasts near the bank of the river, or it is just as likely that a fleet of pirates has come up through some other branch of the river, and has been plundering the villages they have fallen in with, as I have known them often to do in these parts. It wouldn't be safe to fall in with them. They would soon run down our boats and not leave a man of us alive."

"Though you may be mistaken, we will take the prudent course and try to find out who the people are," answered the first mate. "Wake up Kalong, and you and he jump into the canoe and paddle ahead until you have discovered what they are about. Take care, however, that you are not caught yourselves."

Ned awakened the Malay and explained the object we had in view, when the two hauling up the canoe alongside got into her and noiselessly paddled up the river, keeping near the bank where we lay moored.

We waited anxiously listening for any sound, but a light breeze rustling among the trees prevented those we had before heard from reaching our ears.

"Ned, I hope, may have been mistaken, after all," observed the first mate; "it would be a pity, having got this far, to have to give up our expedition; but, as he says, it would never do to run the risk of an encounter with those savage pirates. If he is right we must do our best to avoid them and be ready for a start."

All hands in both boats had been aroused, and we were prepared to heave up our anchors and get out the oars at a moment's notice. We had not only our own safety to think of, but that of our shipmates, if there really was a fleet of pirates in the river, should they discover the brig—ill able to defend herself as she was—they might attack and capture her before we could get on board. We had brought the two boats alongside each other, so that we could talk without raising our voices. The first mate, who had been standing up on the after thwart that he might the better be able to see any object ahead, at length observed, "The canoe ought to have been back by this time. Can she have been taken by the savages?"

"If so, Kalong and Ned may for the sake of saving their lives have told them about the brig," observed the boatswain. "If there is another channel the pirates will go down it and attack her before they look after us."

"I feel very sure that Ned will not prove treacherous, though I cannot say how the Malay will act," I observed.

"At all events we will get up our anchors and be ready for a start," said the first mate.

He gave the order accordingly. Just as they were up to the bows, I caught sight of a small object ahead, which I trusted was the canoe. I pointed it out to the first mate.

"No doubt about it. I hope that we shall find that we might have saved ourselves the trouble of weighing," he observed.

It approached rapidly. In little more than a minute it dropped alongside us and Ned and Kalong leapt into our boat.

"Not a moment to lose!" exclaimed Ned; "there's a whole fleet of prahus in the next reach. Some of the people were ashore, and that we might find out who they were, we landed some way below where they lay and crept up close to them until we could hear them speaking. They know of the brig, and, we found, were just about to get under weigh hoping to surprise her."

"We must be on board first, then, or they'll murder the whole of us. Out oars, lads, and pull as you never pulled before," cried the first mate.

The crews required no further orders, the boats were got round and away we went with the current, the men pulling with all their might.

"We must go on board and fight for our lives, for if we are taken they'll not be worth much," said the first mate.

"My poor father, what will become of him?" I exclaimed.

"We have no proof that your father is among the white men spoken of, Harry. If he is, he will not be worse off than he would have been had we not gone up the river. We must, however, try and ascertain the truth of the report, and make another attempt to rescue him should we find that he is really there."

We had not much time or inclination for talking; while the first mate steered, I kept looking astern to ascertain if we were pursued. We rapidly shot by the places we had slowly passed coming up; we were thankful that we had the tide in our favour. We had got to the end of a long reach, when I saw rounding the further end of the point we had last passed a number of dark objects stretching across the stream. I had no doubt that they were the piratical prahus, though whether they had discovered us or not we could not ascertain. They were swift craft, I knew, and might possibly overtake us before we could reach the brig. There was no use in telling the men to give way, as they were pulling as hard as they could lay their backs to the oars. They saw the enemy too, and knew the horrible fate which would be ours should we be overtaken. We, of course, however, had no intention of yielding as long as we could defend ourselves; we had our arms therefore ready for instant use. Hard as our crews pulled, the prahus appeared to be coming up with us. Every instant they became more distinct, and we had little doubt that they must see us. I had begun to despair of escaping when the first mate raised our spirits by announcing that he saw the light in the brig's rigging in the distance. It was to be hoisted on the fore stay that in case we should return at night we might know where to find her. It was indeed fortunate that this arrangement had been made, or we might have run out to sea without observing her. We now altered our course, hoping that the Malays might possibly shoot by the brig before they discovered that the light was on board her. The first mate hailed the brig as we approached.

"We are pursued by a fleet of pirates. Stand by to hoist in the boats, and to make sail as soon as we are on board."

The captain hailed in reply, "We are on the alert. Pull up one on each quarter."

The moment we got alongside the falls were slackened and we swarmed up them, each man running to the tackles as he got on deck. The boats were quickly hoisted in, when the crew ran aloft to loose the sails. The wind was blowing down the river, but there was barely enough of it to give the vessel steerage way, and without a stronger breeze we should run the risk of drifting on shore. The cable, however, was hove short, and we were ready at a moment's notice to stand out to sea. The dark line of prahus were, however, in the meantime approaching, evidently, by their appearance, with hostile intent.

As they drew nearer the pirates suddenly broke forth into loud cries, sounding their trumpets and beating their gongs and tom-toms, apparently with the intention of frightening us. We had our guns pointed at them and the matches ready to fire the instant the captain issued the order, but he was unwilling if it could be avoided to commence the fight, and waited until they should show their hostile intentions. Of these we were not long left in doubt. They had probably expected to surprise the brig, but now, from having seen the boats ahead, they knew that we should be on the alert. Again bursting forth into shouts and shrieks, and making all the noise they could with their musical instruments, they opened a fire from their gingalls and muskets, followed up by a shower of darts. Although we could hear the missiles come rattling on board, being sheltered by our high bulwarks, no one, as far as I could tell, was hurt.

"Now give it them, lads!" cried the captain. We let fly with all our guns, those having muskets firing them also. We quickly reloaded, to be ready for the enemy should they attempt to board us. When I saw the number of prahus which

　　　　　　　　W. H. G. Kingston

had assembled on all sides, I could not help fearing that we might be overpowered at last. Still the first dose we had given them seemed to have produced a good effect.

"Fire, my lads, and load again as fast as you can," cried the captain. "We must keep them off until we can get the brig under weigh. Hurrah! Here comes a breeze. Quick, quick, give it them!"

We fired another broadside. "Now heave up the anchor and sheet home the topsails," he shouted.

The order was obeyed, and before the pirates had recovered from the dismay into which our last broadside had thrown them, the anchor was hove up to the bows, and the topsails being sheeted home and the mainsail set, we were gliding out towards the mouth of the river, not, however, without being accompanied by our persevering foes.

We had several on either side of us blazing away with their gingalls and hurling darts and spears on our decks. At last one more daring than the rest ran alongside just as we had discharged our two guns, and her crew began climbing on board. The first mate and boatswain and several of the men were ready to receive them, and beat them back with pikes and cutlasses. The rest of our crew were employed in defending the other side, though it was sharp work to keep them back. Several of the pirates were cut down as they showed their heads over the bulwarks, but others climbed up after them. Blyth and I, seeing how hard pressed the first mate was, sprang to his assistance, while the captain was everywhere, now at the helm, now on one side, now on the other, encouraging the crew, slashing away at the pirates, and seeing that the man at the helm was steering as was necessary.

The chief part of the fighting took place between the main and fore chains. Several heads appeared abaft the main rigging, though quickly driven back again by the captain's untiring cutlass, aided by Blyth and me. Every moment we expected other prahus to come up on the opposite side, but they kept away, waiting perhaps until their chief had gained a footing on our deck. Meanwhile our long gun and the two carronades, besides several muskets—with which we kept up a hot fire—contributed to keep them at a respectful distance. The cabin windows had been battened up, but another prahu attempted to throw some men on board by getting under our stern. The captain, however, who was on the watch for this, caught sight of her, and calling to Blyth and me, we used our cutlasses and pikes with such good effect that the enemy was driven back and their prahu fell astern. I was springing off the poop when I caught sight of a man just creeping in through an after port. I was on the point of running at him with my pike, when he cried out—

"A friend, a friend, don't strike!"

It was with the greatest difficulty I avoided doing so. "Whoever you are, get in quickly, that I may close the port, or others will follow," I exclaimed.

He did as I advised, and assisted me in lashing down the port. "I'll do it," he said, "for I don't want to be caught again," and with the quickness of a seaman he secured the port.

"If you give me a cutlass I'll fight for you," he said; and as I handed him mine he sprang to the side and soon made good use of it by cutting down a couple of fellows who had at that moment shown themselves above the bulwarks, while Blyth and I with our pikes drove back two more who were climbing on board. The next instant I heard the first mate

W. H. G. Kingston

singing out—

"They are sheering off! Now give it them, lads! Fire low and we shall send the shot through her bottom."

It took some little time, however, to load the guns, and before they could be fired the prahu had got some fathoms off. The shot, however, took all the better effect, and went crashing through her thin sides. Almost in an instant she filled, when the survivors of her crew attempted to gain the other prahus, which kept on our beam, and now again began to discharge their guns and other missiles at us as before. The breeze, however, was freshening, and we could see that our shot had taken effect on several of the other prahus, which sank as we watched them. Our crew uttered a loud cheer, to show the enemy that they might expect as warm a reception as before should they again attempt to board us. Having now time to set the foresail and topgallant-sails, fast as the Malays pulled, we had every reason to hope that we should get clear of them.

CHAPTER FOUR

The pirates, though so roughly handled, continued hovering on every side, making way with their oars, perhaps hoping that the wind might fall, and should the brig be becalmed that they might attack us with greater advantage than before. Happily, however, the breeze freshened, and we kept up so continuous a fire from our long gun and carronades that they were afraid of approaching nearer.

"Keep it up, my lads," said the captain, "we shall soon give them the go-bye. They'll not wish to pay us another visit."

Soon after this, looking eastward, I saw the first bright streaks of the dawn appearing in the sky. The light rapidly increased; we could now clearly distinguish the prahus dotting the smooth ocean. There were a dozen of them at least, and we had sent two, if not more, to the bottom. I had hitherto been so busily employed in working one of the guns that I had been unable to make any inquiries of the stranger as to who he was or where he had come from. He had been assisting at the aftermost gun until, overcome with fatigue, he had sunk down on the deck just under the poop, where he had remained unnoticed. As our crew saw the pirate fleet dropping astern out of range of our guns they broke into loud cheers, joined in even by those most badly wounded. At the same time the sun, appearing like an arch of fire, rose from behind the distant land, suffusing the whole eastern sky with a ruddy glow, and then rapidly shooting upward, the entire circle made its appearance. I now hurried off to the stranger, followed by the first mate, hoping that he might give us tidings of my father, yet almost dreading to hear what those tidings might be. He tried to rise as we approached, but had scarcely strength left to do so. His countenance was pale, his clothes wet and blood-stained.

Uncle Jack lifted him up and seated him on a gun. "You are hungry and knocked up, my man. When you have had some food you shall tell us where you came from, and how you got on board the brig."

"Thank you, sir. I do want food, and should be glad to get a wound I have in my side looked to, as it is beginning to hurt."

Uncle Jack told me to go and forage in the cabin for such food as I could lay hands on, while he did his best to bind up the man's wound. The second mate and steward, I should have said, were engaged in attending to the hurts of the other men. Strange as it may seem, notwithstanding the numbers of shot, spears, and bullets sent on board us, no one had been killed.

The captain was on the poop, attending to the steering of the brig and watching the proceedings of the enemy.

I soon returned with some ham and bread and a mug of water, and I got from the steward some bandages and salve. While Uncle Jack carefully bound up his wound, the stranger eagerly took a draught of water, and was then able to swallow some of the food I had brought.

We had hitherto restrained our eagerness; but as soon as he

appeared somewhat recovered, my uncle told him how much we wished to hear the account he had to give of himself, adding that we had gone up the river to search for some Englishmen said to be prisoners to the natives.

"We expected to find my father, Captain Musgrave, who lately commanded the 'Amphion,'" I observed.

The stranger's answer at once dispelled my hopes.

"I was one of the Englishmen you heard of, but we were not prisoners. There was another man with me; we belonged to a vessel from Sydney trading with the natives, but having had a quarrel with our skipper, we were left behind. We thought that we could establish a trade with the natives, as my mate had once done in one of the South Sea islands, and we were waiting until another vessel should come up the river. We had been there three years or more, and were becoming accustomed to the life, though we had made up our minds to go away if any vessel appeared. Two nights ago we were sleeping in our house close to the bank of the river, when we were awakened by fearful shrieks and cries. Looking out we saw a number of prahus brought up along the bank, and hundreds of fellows, whom we knew to be pirates, with swords in their hands, rushing about setting fire to the houses and cutting off the heads of the unfortunate people as they tried to escape from the flames. They had not yet discovered our house, but as a party of them drew near we sang out to them, saying that if they wished to be friends with us we were ready to be friends with them; but if not, we were determined to fight to the last, besides which we threatened to set fire to the house and to destroy all the goods within it, but which we offered otherwise to make over to them. We took aim as we spoke at their chief, who appeared at their head. They seemed to think that they might obtain our heads at too high a price if they attacked us; and having held a palaver, the chief promised that if we would come out of our house our lives should be safe. We, knowing very well that though we might kill two or three of them—should they not value our goods they would burn us out in a few minutes— thought it wise to agree to their terms. We told them, however, that we must think over the matter, and if they would leave us in quiet a short time we would give them an answer. As they had killed all the people they could catch, the rest having escaped into the woods, they were perfectly satisfied, I suppose, with their night's work. Leaving a guard to watch us, the rest employed themselves in embarking all the booty they had collected. At last the chief came back, which made us believe that he intended to act fairly—he knew that we could have shot him if we had been so disposed. He now shouted out to us that as he wanted to be off we must make up our minds either to accompany him or be killed. We replied that if we were killed our countrymen would hear of it and punish him some day or other pretty severely. He had heard, I doubt not, of the punishment the pirates had received in the neighbourhood of Sarawak. He swore by the prophet that no harm should happen to us.

"'Well, Charley,' said my mate, Pat Tandy, 'there is no use making more ado about the matter. We shall only put the fellow out of temper. It is our only chance.'"

"I agreed with him, and opening the door of our house, we went down the steps, holding our muskets in our hands ready to have a last shot if we saw that the pirates intended to play us a trick. We walked straight up to the chief and took his hand to show him that we were not afraid. As soon as we were out of the house, the people rushed in and soon carried away the goods, the result of our trading—mats, skins, nuts, and other things. The chief told us that we must give up our muskets, as he wanted them; and as there was nothing said about them in our agreement, we handed them to him, not feeling very sure but that the next moment we might find our heads off our shoulders. However, he was a more honest man in that respect than we took him for.

"He now marched us down to the bank, put Tandy on board his prahu, and I was ordered on board another. We had been so long with the natives that we understood their language. They were pretty free and easy in talking, but we could not make out what they intended to do with us. I suspected, however, that all was not right when they kept us apart, so I made up my mind to escape on the first opportunity, and I had no doubt that Pat would do the same.

"We remained where we were until news was brought that an English merchant vessel had anchored in the mouth of the river, and they, having held a counsel, determined to attack her. I tried to escape, hoping to warn you of your danger, but I was caught, and was threatened if I made another attempt that I should lose my life. You know most of the rest. If the pirates had found you napping, they would have murdered every one of you and plundered your brig. I felt sure, from the way you defended yourselves, that you would gain the victory. I took the opportunity while the Malays were engaged in fighting you to jump overboard and swim to you. Just as I reached the water, a fellow catching sight of me pounded me with his spear, and very nearly hooked me back; but diving, I came up some distance off, and he thought probably that I was drowned. As I could find no means of getting up your side, I clambered on board the prahu, and from her got through the after port, which I found open. What has become of Tandy I cannot say; he may have attempted to follow my example and has lost his life, or, poor fellow! They will kill him when they find I have escaped."

Charley Bell's account of himself was very wonderful, but

we had no reason to disbelieve it.

As he was much hurt, the first mate, who was always ready to sacrifice his own comfort for the good of others, placed him in his own berth that he might the better attend to him. We then went to assist my uncle in looking after the other wounded men. Two were unfit for duty, but the rest managed to get about with bandaged arms and heads, and a somewhat ghastly crew they looked. The second mate and boatswain were slightly hurt, and Blyth had received two wounds, but neither were of much consequence; while the captain, though three bullets had gone through his clothes, was uninjured, as were the first mate and I. On going to the mast-head, I discovered through the spy-glass the pirate fleet far away astern. On hearing this the captain determined to stand out into the sea of Celebes to avoid another encounter with them.

It seemed surprising that although our good captain had been almost confined to his cabin up to the time we entered the river he should have been able to exert himself as he did when the brig was attacked, and still more so that he suffered no ill consequences, but rapidly afterwards regained his health and strength.

Bell told us that had any English vessel been wrecked on the coast he thought he should have heard of it, so that we were tolerably well satisfied that the "Amphion" had not been cast away on the east shore of Borneo.

Captain Haiselden had heard at Singapore that the Dutch sent out numerous men-of-war to cruise round Celebes and the Spice Islands for the purpose of putting down piracy, and as they would have heard of any vessel cast away near the places they were accustomed to visit, he was convinced that the "Amphion" must have been wrecked on some island shore to the northward. He therefore resolved, instead of running through the Straits of Macassar, to continue east-ward across the sea of Celebes and ultimately rounding the Moluccas, to sail down the coast of New Guinea. The weather continued remarkably fine, the air was pure, though not cool, and the wounded men, who were on deck as much as possible, rapidly recovered.

The first place at which it was arranged we should touch was at the northern end of the curiously shaped island of Celebes. A strong southerly wind, which afterwards shifted to the south-east, springing up, compelled us to keep more to the northward than we should otherwise have done.

It was night, we were steering to the eastward but intended soon to put about, expecting on the next tack to reach Menado, when just at daybreak we found that we were close to an island with a lofty conical peak and lower ground to the southward of it. The chart showed us that it was the island of Sanguir. A current must have set us towards it, for we supposed that we were some distance off. We at once put about, when the wind dropped and we lay perfectly becalmed on the mirror-like deep. I could not perceive the slightest swell, nor did even a cat's-paw play over the surface. I threw some chips into the water, and when I looked some hours afterwards there they were, floating like little boats alongside. The smoke from the galley-fire curled upwards in a thin blue wreath, growing thinner and thinner until it became invisible far over head. Now and then a flying-fish would break through the glassy surface, or some monster of the deep show us his snout, leaving a circle of wavelets as he quickly descended. It was even hotter below than on deck, and every piece of metal felt as if just taken from the furnace. The seams of the deck spluttered and hissed, and as we walked about the pitch stuck to our feet. There was nothing, however, in the sky which betokened a hurricane, while the barometer continued as high as usual.

W. H. G. Kingston

"I believe it is only an ordinary calm," observed the captain to the first mate, as they stood under the shade of the mainsail, which hung down without giving a single lazy flap.

"It might, however, be better to take in our light canvas in case a sudden squall should strike us," observed Uncle Jack. "It will give the hands something to do, and we can easily make sail again should a breeze spring up."

"I hope that we may get one before long, for we are drifting in faster than I like to the land; we will get the cable ranged ready to bring up should it become necessary. The wind when it comes may blow off shore, but it may blow on it and we shall be compelled to anchor."

"If we can find sufficiently shallow water outside the breakers," observed Uncle Jack, as he stepped out from under the shelter of the sail to give the orders he had received.

Having sprung aloft, I had just assisted in furling the main-topgallant-sails and had returned on deck, when I felt the brig give a heave and suddenly tremble throughout her frame for several seconds. We cast inquiring looks at each other, wondering what could have happened. The first mate, taking a lead-line, hove it overboard, thinking it possible that the vessel had struck a reef.

"No bottom!" he exclaimed in a tone of satisfaction. "What can it be?"

"Little doubt about that," observed the captain, "an earthquake is taking place, see what's happening there," and he pointed to the island.

As he spoke a dense volume of smoke, followed by ruddy

flames, was seen to ascend from the summit of the cone, while the whole island—from which a dull rumbling sound came off—seemed for a moment to heave. We turned out glasses towards it. All was quiet, but presently we saw the trees waving to and fro, as if shaken by a hurricane, while vast masses of rock rolled down from the summits of the hills into the valleys below. Every instant the eruption from the volcano was increasing. In a short time the sky became shrouded by a dense black cloud. Showers of fine cinders fell on our decks, covering also the hitherto blue ocean with a black scum. A red mass of lava bubbled up, as if from some mighty cauldron, above the edge of the crater, and fiery streams began to flow down the sides of the mountain, some taking a course towards the ocean, others making their way in the direction of the valleys, threatening to seize in their course on the tall trees, those near the summit being quickly ablaze. With fearful rapidity the conflagration spread, up the hills, across the plains, sweeping over the plantations and destroying the dwellings of the unfortunate inhabitants. It seemed impossible that a single human being could escape. For some hours we watched the dreadful scene.

"If you will give me leave, sir, I'll go in and try to save some of the poor people," said the first mate. "It seems to me that we might approach yonder point without risk. I see a village a short distance inland, and that cannot long escape destruction, so that the people will try to escape to the point, and we might take off some of them. Others may be saved on board their own craft lying in the harbour to the southward. As far as I can make out there are no boats abreast of us."

"Be quick about it, then, Radburn, for we must not leave the brig short-handed," said the captain.

Blyth and I at once volunteered to go, as did Ned and Bell, thus leaving the vessel with her full complement of men. A boat was lowered and away we pulled. The ashes continued to fall, and the oppressive heat made it difficult to breathe. We pulled on, anxious to save as many of our fellow-creatures as we could. As we approached the point we saw a number of persons rushing towards the end, carrying all sorts of articles on their backs, and others following. Good reason they had to hasten, for the woods at the back of the village were already blazing furiously, and in another minute it would be in flames.

"We must allow only a dozen to enter the first boat," said Uncle Jack; "if more are taken on board we shall run the risk of being swamped. It seems cruel to those left behind, but we must be determined, and try to make another trip."

As we got nearer, so heavily did the surf break on the extreme end of the point, that it seemed scarcely possible we ourselves should escape destruction. On getting in closer, however, we discovered a bay into which we could run. As soon as the people saw the boat, they rushed towards us holding out their arms. We told Bell to shout to them and say that we could take only a few at a time, but would return for the rest, and that we must save the women and children first. The men did not seem to understand this, and we literally had to drive them back, while we dragged in the poor women, mostly with infants or young children in their arms. With these we could carry many more, and we got on board upwards of twenty. Those who remained shrieked and cried, wringing their hands and pointing to the flames as we shoved off.

We bent to our oars as well as we could, crowded as the boat was, and made our way back to the brig. The crew stood ready to haul the poor people upon deck.

"You might venture to send another boat, sir," cried Uncle

Jack; "there is no sign of wind, and many more might be saved."

He did not stop, however, for the captain's answer, but the moment the women and children were out of the boat away we pulled again for the land. We had not got far when, to my satisfaction, I saw that another boat had been lowered, and before we reached the shore she overtook us, under the charge of Mr Crowfoot.

Uncle Jack warned him not to overload his boat. We followed the same plan as before, taking in this time several men, which brought the boat down deep in the water, although we had fewer persons on board than on the first trip. It was piteous to hear the cries of the poor wretches we were compelled to leave behind. Their village had disappeared, and the flames were seizing on every tree and bush up to the inner part of the rocky point. At any moment a fiery shower might come falling down and envelope them. The heat was greater than ever, and the dust and ashes, which came showering down upon upon us, almost overpowering. Uncle Jack, thinking only of saving life, scarcely heeded this. Again we pulled back to the brig.

"You have done enough, Radburn. Your lives will be endangered if you return," cried the captain.

"Only one more trip! Just let me take one more trip, sir," answered the first mate.

The captain could not refuse. The boatswain followed us. We reached the little bay in safety. As I looked up at the mountain I saw that the eruption had become more violent than ever. The lurid flames, casting a light over the whole bland, enabled us to see objects as clearly as in the day-time. We were engaged in taking the people in, our boat was almost full, when Uncle Jack cried out, hauling in another poor man as he did so.

"Shove off, pull away for your lives, my lads!"

Looking up for an instant I saw that a fresh outbreak of the mountain was taking place. Stones, cinders, and ashes came bursting through the air, and crashing down not many hundred yards it seemed from where we lay. The ocean, too, was fearfully agitated, and wave upon wave with loud roars rolled towards the beach. The people on shore stretched out their arms imploring us to take them in, but we could not save them. Had we attempted it our destruction would have been inevitable. The boat's head had been got round, and we pulled as we had never pulled before. The fearful shower rapidly increased. A boiling sea washed over the point, and the hapless beings who stood there disappeared. Not a cry was heard, their death had been instantaneous. Even those who had endeavoured to escape by swimming must have been in a moment overwhelmed. Fast as we pulled, the shower of ashes from the mountain seemed to be following us still faster, and we could see that the shower stretched away even towards the ship.

Happily the calm continued, and we succeeded in getting on board. The poor people we had rescued, while profuse in expressing their thanks to us, gave vent to their grief at the loss of their relations and friends. We understood also from them that there were other villages in the interior, which, with all their inhabitants, must have been utterly destroyed.

We afterwards heard that two thousand persons perished. The people on board were of the Malay race, and, except through our interpreters, Ned and Charley, we could not understand a word they said; indeed, the two seamen could only partly make out their language. We ourselves were not altogether satisfied with our position. A strong wind might spring up and drive us on shore, and we were still so near the volcano that it might cover us, not only with ashes, but with huge masses of rock and stones, which might come crashing down upon us and send us to the bottom. All hands were on deck ready to trim sails the moment the wind should come. We had not long to wait. A loud rushing sound was heard. The canvas gave several loud flaps. The captain had feared that the heat from the burning island might draw the wind towards us. So it did, but, happily for us, it came from the north-west, though we could not tell to what quarter it might suddenly shift.

The yards were braced up on the starboard tack, and we stood away from the island, with the blazing forests on our port-quarter.

The captain's great object now was to get a good offing from Sanguir. He did not intend to bear up for Menado until daylight. It was important that we should reach it without delay to land our passengers, as they would soon exhaust our water and provisions. We did our best to attend to the poor people, but they would not be comforted. They thought of their homes and relatives destroyed, and knew not what hardships they might have to endure. As we got to a distance from the island we could see far away to the southward another bright blaze which rose from the volcano of Sias, also in a state of eruption. On looking at the chart we saw that there was a line of many others, some in the northern end of Celebes, others in Gillolo, extending northward and all the way round to the west through Java. We could only hope that those in the direction to which we were steering might not also burst forth. The wind continued favourable and moderate. When the people heard from Ned where we were going they were in a great fright, declaring that the inhabitants were "head hunters," and that they should all

W. H. G. Kingston

be killed.

When Ned told me this I inquired of the captain if they had any foundation for their fears. He replied that formerly the inhabitants of that part of Celebes were as savage as those of other portions, but that the Dutch have used every possible means to civilise them by giving them employment, introducing commerce, establishing schools, and sending missionaries among them, and that thus a wilderness, inhabited by naked savages, who were wont to garnish their rude houses with human heads, had been converted into a smiling region, with a civilised community.

The next day we made the northern end of Celebes, for which we were steering, and before dark anchored off the pretty little town of Menado. As we looked at it from our anchorage we could see rows of rustic houses, with broad paths between them forming streets, mostly at right angles with each other.

In several directions roads branched off towards the interior, also lined by a succession of cottages surrounded by gardens and plantations. The captain and Blyth immediately went on shore to visit the President or Governor, who, on hearing what had happened, allowed us to land our passengers, promising to look after them, and give them plenty of employment if they were inclined to labour. We were thankful to get them out of the brig, and their fears being dissipated when they saw the civilised state of the country, they thanked us for the kindness shown them, and we parted good friends.

We afterwards called on an English merchant long settled here, who assured us that the people would be well cared for and sent back should they wish it to Sanguir, when information could be received that the volcano was once more at rest. The chief production of the district is coffee, of which we shipped a considerable quantity as freight. We found the account given by the captain in no way exaggerated, and we could easily believe, as asserted, that the inhabitants are the most industrious, peaceable, and civilised, that they are better educated, better clothed, better housed, and better fed of any of the natives of the vast archipelago. Commerce, a paternal, though somewhat despotic Government, and education, combined with Christian missionary effort, has worked the wonderful change in less than forty years. Our friend, who had a house in the country, took Mr Blyth and me up to see his plantations, as also a menagerie which he had formed. In passing a piece of open ground we caught sight of a number of animals, which I supposed to be dogs. They were making their way towards an orchard.

"The rascals!" exclaimed our friend, "they are on a predatory expedition, intending to steal the fruit from yonder trees."

Jumping off his horse, and taking his gun, which his servant carried, he ran towards them. They did not appear to notice him until he was within shot of them. He fired, when one fell and the rest took to flight, quickly scrambling up the trees of the forest, which extended towards us to within a short distance where they were lost to sight. On examining the creature he had killed I found it to be about the size of a spaniel, of a jet black colour, with the projecting dog-like muzzle and overhanging brows of a baboon. It had large callosities, and a scarcely visible tail, not an inch in length.

Our friend told us that these creatures were monkeys, though more like baboons, that descending from the trees where they live, they often invade orchards and gardens, and commit great havoc. Our friend's house was something like an Indian bungalow, though of rougher materials, and was surrounded by a fine garden and orchard, with extensive

W. H. G. Kingston

plantations in the rear. I cannot describe more than two of the animals in his menagerie. One was the Tapiutan, which from its appearance I could not say whether it should be called a cow, a buffalo, or an antelope. It was of the size of a very small Highland cow, and had long straight horns, which were ringed at the base, and sloped backwards over the neck.

The strangest animal he showed us was called the Babirusa, which resembled in general appearance a pig, but it had long and slender legs, and tusks curved upwards so as to look like horns. Those of the lower jaw were long and sharp, but the upper ones grew upwards out of bony sockets through the skin on each side of the snout, curving backwards to near the eyes, and were ten inches long. Our friend told us that it is found over the whole island. He supposed the object of the curling tusks was to preserve the eyes of the animal when searching for the fallen fruits on which it lives among the tangled thickets of spring plants. Though the female does not possess them, perhaps the male gallantly clears the way for her so as to render them unnecessary. However, I must not stop to give a longer description of this interesting place, or many others we saw; I indeed made only two trips ashore, as I had to be on board attending to my duty.

CHAPTER FIVE

Once more the anchor was weighed, and we were about to stand out of the picturesque bay of Menado the moment a boat, in which Mr Blyth had gone on shore to bring off a supply of fresh provisions, returned.

Ned, who had been one of the crew, as soon as the sails were set, came up to me. "I've just heard something, sir, which may or may not be of importance," he said. "I was talking to one of the men we brought off from Sanguir, when he confessed to me that he had been on board the prahu which took me off the shore where we were wrecked. I think he spoke the truth when he told me how I kicked when the pirates made me take an oar and pull with the black fellows they had, I suppose, made slaves of. I asked him if he could tell me where the place was. He answered that it was on the shores of a large island—a very large one, I should think, and away somewhere to the eastward, for he pointed in that direction, though I could not make out exactly how far off it was."

I was deeply interested, and told him that he ought to have brought the man on board that we might have examined him more particularly with the aid of Bell and Kalong.

"He would have been afraid to trust himself, sir," answered

W. H. G. Kingston

Ned; "as he owned that he had been a pirate, he was afraid that the captain or the Dutch might punish him."

I immediately communicated what I had heard to the first mate, who told the captain. They sent for Ned, who, as he said that he had got all the information he could out of the Malay, they did not propose putting back, as I fancied they would have done. I do not think that the captain was sanguine about finding any of the "Amphion's" crew, though Uncle Jack kept up his hopes and mine.

"It may be like looking for a needle in a bundle of hay; still, if we search long enough, the needle will be found," he remarked. "As long as the captain will agree we will continue the search."

Rounding the northern end of Celebes, we crossed the Molucca passage for Ternate, where we were to call. It is a small island off the coast of the large but little known one of Gillolo. As we approached we saw rising out of the sea in a line several conical-shaped mountains, four thousand feet in height, one of which the captain said was Ternate, for which we were bound. Passing between that island and Tidore, of even greater height, we anchored before the town which stretches along the shore, while the mountain overhanging it was clothed to a considerable height with trees and spice plantations. The scenery was truly magnificent, but as we thought of the eruption of Sanguir, we saw in what a moment the whole town and neighbourhood might be reduced to desolation should an eruption burst forth from the mountains which rose so grandly above our heads. We remained here four days, during which an earthquake—an event of frequent occurrence—took place.

I grudged every moment's delay, and was thankful when we once more were steering southward. We were sailing on with a light breeze through a perfectly smooth sea, when a dull roaring sound was heard, like a heavy surf astern. The roar rapidly increased, and we saw a white line of foam rolling on. Thinking that it might be the precursor of a hurricane, we clewed up the topsails, but as the wave passed we rode easily over it with the same sort of movement which is felt when entering a river across a bar. It was followed with a short interval by another of similar character, succeeded with greater rapidity by ten or twelve more, when the sea became as smooth as before. The captain had no doubt that these waves were caused by an earthquake occurring at some distance to the northward. While at Ternate we heard that a suspicious fleet of large prahus had been seen steering to the southward. It was intended, should a Dutch man-of-war arrive, to send her to watch their proceedings. We were advised to keep a sharp look-out for the pirates, and avoid them if we could. "If they think you are Dutch, they'll be cautious how they molest you; but if they suppose that you belong to any other nation, they are very likely to try and plunder you, as they are aware that no men-of-war except those of the Dutch are accustomed to cruise in these seas," said our friend, an English merchant residing in the place.

Captain Haiselden thanked his informant, and replied that we had already fallen in with such gentry, and knew how to deal with them.

"But these are larger and more formidable craft than those by which you were before attacked. If they once get alongside your brig, you will find it a difficult matter to beat them off," was the reply.

Wherever we touched we made inquiries about the "Amphion," but as yet we had only the information gained through Ned from the Sanguir Malay to guide us. She might have been lost at Gillolo itself, and yet the Dutch might not have heard of it, as but very irregular intercourse is kept up between the different parts of that little known island.

Proceeding south we passed between the islands of Bouro and Ceram, calling at Amboina and Banda, spice islands belonging to the Dutch.

We were steering to the east when land was sighted from the mast-head on the starboard bow. I went aloft. It was a small island, one of many extending directly across our course. Intending to pass to the northward of it we luffed up a little, when, after standing on some way further, I was again sent to the mast-head, to see if I could discover any intervening coral reefs or any others running out from it. I could discover no variation of colour in the sea to indicate the existence of hidden reefs in our course, but my eye fell on a dark object, a mile, or it may have been less, from the shore. At the first glance I thought it was a rock rising out of the water, but on descending to the cross-trees and looking through my glass I saw that the object was a ship on a reef, heeling over to one side, with, as far as I could make out, her topmasts, if not her lower masts, gone; at all events she had no canvas set. On coming down to the deck, I told the first mate, who had charge of the watch, and he went aloft and had a look at her also.

"She's in a dangerous position, and I fear is wrecked," he observed. "We must get up to her, and try to render her assistance. If she's not to be got off, we shall have to take her people on board."

"Has she been driven by a gale on the reef, do you think?" I asked.

"No; I should say that she was brought up by it, and that the tide has since fallen, leaving her in her present position, so that when it rises she may be got off."

While we were speaking the sails gave several flaps against the masts, a sign that the wind had suddenly fallen, and we lay becalmed. This was the more tantalising as we were anxious to go to the assistance of the ship.

I went below to inform the captain, who at once came on deck, and, after looking round the horizon, said that he thought a breeze would soon again spring up, and that we would then stand towards the ship and see what we could do, adding, "in the meantime, as the tide rises she may probably haul off without our assistance."

"I should like to take one of the boats and pull on board her," observed Uncle Jack.

"As it must be several hours before you could be back again, the weather might in the meantime change; so that I cannot consent to your going," answered the captain, in a tone which prevented the first mate from making a reply.

Still Uncle Jack, not satisfied, walked the deck uneasily. He wished at once to relieve the anxiety of those on board the ship by letting them know that assistance was near should they not have observed the brig.

Hour after hour passed by, darkness came on, and still no breeze ruffled the surface of the ocean. All night long the calm continued.

As soon as daylight broke, I was again aloft looking out for the ship. There she lay in the same position as before; it was evident that whatever exertions had been made to get her off, they had been unsuccessful. I was about to come on deck again, when, sweeping my glass round to the northward, I made out another island of large size apparently. Between it and where the ship lay I fancied that I could distinguish a number of small black dots, so faint, however, that had I not steadied my glass, which was a very good one, I should not have observed them. Recollecting what we had heard about the pirate fleet, a fear seized me at once that they might be prahus, and that they were on their way to pillage the wreck, which they must have discovered while lying off the northern island. Whether they had discovered us it was impossible to say, but they certainly would do so when the sun rose and shone on our canvas.

I at once came down and told the first mate, who took a hurried glance round the horizon in the hopes of discovering the signs of a coming breeze.

"I must get the captain to let me take a boat to warn the crew of the ship of their danger, and to assist them if they are attacked," he exclaimed. "We may get there before the prahus, which do not pull as fast as they can sail, and a few well-armed men may turn the scale against them; but I'll have a look at them first."

Taking the glass he sprang aloft. Directly afterwards the captain appeared and asked him what he was looking at. I told him.

"I hope we shall get a breeze, for if the pirates, as I suppose they are, see us boldly standing towards them, they will hesitate before they meddle with the wreck," he remarked, now apparently as anxious about the vessel on shore as we had been. "It may have a good effect if we hoist a pendant and the Dutch flag and fire a gun. They will take us for a man-of-war, and probably be off again as fast as they can pull; but it is the breeze we want, the breeze! Without that we are helpless."

The first mate soon came down from aloft and again proffered his request.

"I dare not give you leave," answered the captain. "What could one or even two boats do against those prahus, with twenty or thirty well-armed men in each? You might be cut off, even before you could reach the wreck; and if you were on board, you would be able to do but little to defend her, as in the position she lies she could not work her guns if she had any."

I was almost surprised at the way Uncle Jack pleaded to be allowed to go.

"It is impossible," replied the captain, "I could not reconcile it to my conscience. We might lose half the ship's company, and be unable to defend the brig ourselves."

I never saw the first mate so put out as he was at this answer. He turned away and continued walking the deck with uneasy strides until he seemed almost beside himself. He again went aloft and stood watching the prahus through his glass, occasionally turning his eye round the horizon, and then he shouted, "A breeze! A breeze coming up from the south-west!" The next instant down he slid on deck.

The vessel's head, which had been turning now to one point of the compass now to another, was fortunately just then turned in the right way.

The captain kept a sharp look-out in the direction from whence the wind was coming, to judge whether it was likely to be a strong or a light breeze.

"Set the royals, Radburn. We need not be afraid of it."

The order was quickly obeyed. Scarcely were the sails sheeted home than they blew gently out. The topgallant-sails did the same; the topsails soon filled. The brig gathering way steered a little to the northward so as to intercept the prahus.

We were thankful for the breeze, but we would rather have avoided a struggle.

"You'll have the studding-sails set, sir?" said Uncle Jack, scarcely waiting for an answer before he gave the order, and sprang forward to assist in carrying it out.

We soon had the studding-sails below and aloft, still the brig did not move along as rapidly as we wished. By this time the pirates might have seen us, as the sun was shining brightly on our royals and topgallant-sails, though we could not make them out except from aloft.

We were not long in manufacturing a Dutch pennant, which was run up to the main-royal mast-head. It was doubtful, however, whether it would be seen, or, if seen, have the effect we hoped for. The pirates, observing how light the wind was, would know that they could pull away beyond our reach.

Again and again Uncle Jack went aloft, until we got near enough to distinguish not only the ship on the reef but the prahus from the deck, which were approaching fearfully near her; the guns were loaded and the small arms got ready for immediate use. Most of the men were ready enough for a fight, if a fight was to take place, but the second mate looked downcast as usual, and I heard him muttering—

"We have enough to do to look after ourselves, without fighting for other people."

This was said for the first mate to hear, but Uncle Jack turned away without making any observation.

The prahus, although we must have been seen, still continued their course. Sometimes the hope came across me that they might not be intending to attack the ship ashore; but it was scarcely to be thought that they were going to render her assistance. As we examined them through our glasses, we could see that they were large war prahus with numerous crews. The breeze filled our sails, but continued light as at first, and we had done all that was possible to make the brig move through the water.

Two prahus, apparently the fastest, were leading, and were already scarcely more than two miles off, while we were at a much greater distance. They would be up to the ship in twenty minutes or so, and it would take them but a fearfully short time to perform their work of murder and pillage if they were so minded. Still we hoped that the crew would fight, and, at all events, keep them at bay until we could come up. The pirates were calculating, it was evident, on the wind falling, of which there appeared every probability. Several times the lower canvas had given some ominous flaps against the masts, while the studding-sails hung down from the booms emptied of wind; still the royals filled and forced the brig along.

Our glasses were constantly turned, now towards the ship on shore, now towards the pirate fleet. It showed great hardihood on the part of the Malays that they should still continue their course, while our vessel, which they must have supposed to be a man-of-war, was so close to them. They were trusting, we thought, to their numbers, and to the rapidity with which they could make their escape among the coral reefs, where no sailing vessel could follow them. They were getting closer and closer, while we were making scarcely two knots an hour through the water. What means of defence the ship might possess we could not tell. Even if she had guns she would, as the captain remarked, be unable to work them with her deck inclined as it now was. We could only hope that the tide was rising, and that if so she might get on an even keel, although her crew might not be able to haul her off.

We carried, I should have said, a light whale boat, remarkable for her speed; she pulled four oars, and held three persons besides. The wind provokingly tantalised us, now it filled the sails and then again allowed them to hang loosely down from the yards.

I had gone forward with the first mate that we might watch the ship and the headmost of the prahus. He several times sent me aft that I might take a look astern to see if there were any signs of the breeze increasing. On each occasion I had to make the same report.

"She's lifting, she's lifting?" exclaimed Uncle Jack, at length; "see, she's making signals. Run, Harry, and get the signal book, we will try and learn what she is saying."

I quickly returned with the book, but the wind was so light that the flags did not blow out. "A breath of air for a single moment would enable us to see what they are," observed the first mate, watching them through his telescope. Just then one flag flew out, it was to signify that the others made the number of the ship. I turned to the right place in the signal book; presently all the flags flew out together, it was but for an instant. The first mate rapidly turned over the pages.

"I feared so from the first," he exclaimed; "the captain cannot refuse to let me go, she is the 'Iris.' The pirates have a current against them, or they would have made faster progress. We'll get on board before them yet. Who will volunteer, lads?"

Several of the men replied, "I'm ready!"

We hurried aft, and he entreated the captain to let him have the whale boat. At first I thought the captain was going to refuse.

"We may still hope to be up in time to attack the prahus, and they will not long stand the fire from our guns," he answered. "I don't like to risk your life and those of the people you may take with you."

"I'll take care that we are not caught by them, and I hope that we shall get on board before they can reach the ship," said the first mate.

"Remember, Radburn, the lives of the boat's crew are committed to your charge, and though I shall be glad to help Captain Bingley, you must turn back rather than risk an encounter in the boat with the pirates."

"I will do as you order, sir," answered Uncle Jack, eagerly springing to the falls and singing out for volunteers.

The captain, however, would positively allow only four hands to go, including Ned and Bell, another Englishman, and a Malay. I entreated that I might accompany him, and Blyth volunteered. The captain gave me leave, though Uncle Jack hesitated. Several more of the men came aft.

"It cannot be," said the captain, "we must keep hands enough to fight the brig."

While the boat was being lowered, arms were collected; each man stuck a brace of pistols in his belt, and we had muskets,

W. H. G. Kingston

cutlasses, and several pikes. The captain would not allow us to take more, observing justly that they might be required on board the brig. We really had no reason to complain of his readiness to assist out friends. Not a minute had elapsed before we were ready, and getting out the oars away we pulled, the first mate, of course, steering.

We steered slightly to the south as the current was setting north, which of course made the distance longer. I could not help confessing to myself that it was very doubtful whether we should reach the ship before the prahus.

While the mate steered, Blyth and I employed ourselves in loading the arms. Our men pulled as hard as they could bend their backs to the oars. They believed that if we could once gain the ship's deck, that we should succeed in driving back the pirates as well as we had done on board the brig. We could not tell whether we had been seen from the prahus, but those on board the ship would, we hoped, make out the signal hoisted at the mast-head of the "Lily," that a boat was coming to their assistance, and that this would encourage them to defend themselves should they be attacked before we could reach them. I had never before felt the intense anxiety I now experienced, and I knew how Uncle Jack must be feeling.

We were now rapidly nearing both the leading prahus and the ship, and we could even distinguish the fighting men on the decks of the former, with their gingalls and muskets or spears in their hands, though we could not make out whether they had any guns in their bows.

Captain Bingley had laughed at our carrying so many guns, and Uncle Jack said that when the "Iris" sailed she had only two six-pounders for firing signals. Whether others had afterwards been shipped he could not tell; even the two small ones it was possible might have been hove overboard to lighten the ship.

As I before said the tide was rising, and we remarked that the "Iris" had lifted considerably since we left the brig. I need not say that I very often turned my eyes towards the "Lily" to see if she was moving faster than before. Though still gliding on through the smooth water, it was at a slow pace. Already the leading prahus were within a quarter of a mile of the ship, when their crews ceased rowing. In a short time we saw that it was only to allow some of the others to come up, apparently that they might make their attack together. The delay was of advantage to us. We were near enough to see our friends, who had been anxiously watching us, waving signals from the forecastle. They of course knew who we were. I thought I saw two female dresses. I could hardly be mistaken. But presently they disappeared; probably Captain Bingley had ordered his wife and daughter below to be out of the way of any missiles the pirates might discharge.

"We shall do it, we shall do it. Give way, my fine lads!" cried Uncle Jack; and the crew pulled until I feared they might spring their oars.

We had another danger to encounter, that of running on any intervening coral reefs, and the first mate stood up that he might obtain as far a view as possible ahead. I had been so engaged in watching the prahus, that I had not for some minutes looked at the brig.

"Hurrah!" I shouted, "she's got the breeze at last, and is coming on bravely."

"Thank heaven!" exclaimed Uncle Jack.

At that moment the fighting men on board two of the prahus,

W. H. G. Kingston

which had again got ahead of the others, began firing away at the ship. Not a shot was returned from her. This made me fear that she had no means of defence. On we dashed; even now we might be on board before the prahus got alongside. We were, it should be understood, approaching on the port bow, towards which, for obvious reasons, the mate had steered. The next instant we had hooked on, ladders and ropes were lowered down to enable us to get on board.

"Hoist in the boat, or the pirates may get her!" I heard Captain Bingley shout out.

She was dropped under the davits. We found only, besides Captain Bingley and the mates, half a dozen of the men with firearms, the others had either pikes or boat-hooks, or such weapons as might serve for a hand-to-hand tussle, but could not have prevented the pirates from boarding. We had no time to ask questions, for two of the prahus were almost alongside; hurrying across the deck, we stood with our muskets pointed at them, telling Ned to shout in a loud voice and threaten them with a fearful retribution should they attack us. As they still came on we fired a well-aimed volley at the two nearest, bringing several of their warriors to the deck, while we quickly again loaded. In another instant they might have been attempting to clamber up the sides of the ship, when the people on board the other prahus saw the approach of the brig, which almost immediately opened fire with her long gun run out through her bow port. A panic on this seized most of the fleet, and pulling round away they went, leaving their leaders to their fate. The latter seeing themselves deserted, cast off and pulled away with all their might, their object being to avoid the which continued firing her long gun as fast as it could be loaded. We and the crew of the "Iris" raised a loud cheer as we saw that we had driven off our foes. Though we had had happily but little fighting, Uncle Jack had no doubt by his promptitude saved the ship from being boarded, when in a few minutes every one belonging to her might have been put to death.

Captain Bingley, hurrying up to Uncle Jack and grasping his hand, exclaimed—

"You have saved our lives, Radburn. I thank you from my heart, and there are those below who desire to thank you too."

He then thanked Blyth and me, and our boat's crew, who undoubtedly deserved it from the way they had pulled.

I found that a cable had been carried out astern, and that preparations had been made for hauling off the ship at high water, which, as the sea had remained perfectly calm, the captain hoped to do without her having suffered material damage. She was now rapidly regaining her perpendicular position, and in a few minutes would be on an even keel. The brig, after following the pirates for a short distance, had hove to Captain Haiselden had no fancy for running in among the rocks.

Jack Radburn was soon on deck. "They are all right, I am thankful to say," he observed to me; "they want to thank you and Mr Blyth as soon as you can go below, for coming to their assistance."

By this time, the tide having risen, the ship was once more perfectly upright. The capstan palls were shipped, away we tramped round and round, straining every nerve. In vain we hove, the cable was strained to its utmost, but not an inch did we move. I saw the captain and his mates making long faces as if they thought that the ship was irretrievably lost. Uncle Jack cheered on the men. Already all the water had been started, and some of the heavy part of the cargo.

W. H. G. Kingston

"Never fear, lads," he shouted, "we must heave a few more packages overboard if we don't move soon; but try again, lads, try again."

We pressed against the capstan bars with all our might. Just then I felt her start.

"She moves, she moves!" burst from every mouth.

I shall never forget the delight we felt. Round went the capstan bars. Again and again we cheered.

We were dragging her off, it must be understood, stern first, exactly as she had come on, so that had any coral points existed they must have been torn away. By persevering, in a few minutes she was afloat; and by means of a hawser secured to the cable, it was brought round to the bows, and the ship rode safely at anchor.

CHAPTER SIX

On finding the ship afloat the crew in their joy shook hands all round. There was enough work, however, to be done. The carpenter first sounded the well.

No more water than usual was found in her. It was hoped, therefore, that she had not received any material damage. We had, however, to get up the topmasts and topgallant-masts, the yards across, to weigh the anchors and guns, which had been hove overboard, and no end of other work to accomplish.

We had not been long at anchor before the "Lily," furling sails, brought up a short distance outside of us, and Captain Haiselden with a boat's crew came on board. In spite of the hot sun, we worked hard all day, Uncle Jack, as may be supposed, setting us a good example. Grace, though pale from the alarm she had endured, was as blooming as ever. "Why, I shouldn't have known you," she said, looking at me and coming up to shake hands; "Mamma and I are so grateful to you for the assistance you brought us."

She also thanked Mr Blyth in the same way, I saw that her eye was ranging over the deck in search of Uncle Jack, who was working as hard as any of the men to get the ship to rights.

As the weather was fine we remained at anchor during the night, keeping a very bright look-out lest the pirates might come back; but impressed with the idea that the brig was a Dutch man-of-war, without dreaming of again attacking us, they were probably making the best of their way to the northward, to escape the pursuit they expected. By evening the next day the ship was all *ataunto*. Captain Haiselden, who had returned to the "Lily," again came on board to hold a consultation as to our future proceedings. The "Iris," having started most of her water, had before she could venture any distance from the land to procure a fresh supply. The island on which she had been so nearly wrecked afforded none. The nearest places at which it certainly could be obtained were either at Banda, to the west, or the coast of New Guinea to the east, which was still much nearer.

Captain Bingley proposed sailing west for Banda, but when Captain Haiselden told him that we had on board a man belonging to the "Amphion," who stated that she had not been wrecked in the way described by Howlett and Trinder, but had been driven on the shore of a large island to the eastward, he exclaimed—

"Then, after all, that may have been the remains of the 'Amphion' herself, which we fancied we saw not a week ago, driven in among the rocks on the coast of New Guinea."

He told us that the current had carried the "Iris" in with the coast much closer than he intended to go; while endeavouring to haul off, under a press of sail, one of the hands aloft declared that he saw what looked like a vessel with her masts gone, inside a reef over which she must have been driven. The mates had both gone aloft. The one agreed that the man was right, the other, who looked as the first had done, through a telescope, declaring that "although very like the shattered hull of a ship, it was only a rock of a peculiar shape." As the safety of the "Iris" depended upon her clawing off the shore, it had been impossible to make any further examination, and he had been inclined to think that those who fancied they had seen a wreck were mistaken. At all events, if any of her crew had escaped on shore, he was not in a position to render them any assistance. I watched Uncle Jack's countenance as Captain Bingley was speaking. I guessed what was passing in his mind, though he said nothing then.

"I wouldn't have passed a spot where I thought our countrymen were in slavery without trying to help them," he remarked to me shortly afterwards. "We must go there, Harry, if Captain Bingley refuses to come; our captain will I am sure do his best to visit the spot. I don't blame Captain Bingley, with his wife and daughter on board, for not making the attempt to ascertain if that was really a wreck, though he might have got a safe offing and then sent in a boat."

When Captain Bingley heard of the possibility of the wreck being the "Amphion," he at once agreed to accompany the "Lily" to the neighbourhood of the spot, and to make every effort to try and rescue any of the crew who might be found on shore.

I rather suspect Grace and Mrs Bingley being present greatly influenced him. Not to run the risk of remaining at anchor in so dangerous a place another night, we returned on board the "Lily," when both the brig and ship made sail to the north-east, a course which would carry us close to where the wreck had been seen.

According to the charts, not far off was a bay which had been visited by ships, where abundance of good water could be found. It was agreed, should we discover a harbour, where it was said one existed, that we would anchor within it and send the boats along the coast to the neighbourhood of the wreck.

On the morning of the fourth day after the "Iris" had been got afloat, land was sighted on the starboard bow, as also right ahead, extending from the east a considerable distance to the west, forming apparently a point running out from New Guinea.

Captain Bingley made a signal that the wreck was somewhere abreast of us, but he advised that we should stand into the harbour as proposed. Approaching nearer we made out several channels apparently between islands, inside of which we might at all events find good anchorage. Captain Haiselden offered to lead the way, and shortening sail, with the lead going, we stood on.

The water was deep, the hills rising on either side of us covered with the richest vegetation. Rounding a point we presently found ourselves in a beautiful land-locked harbour, from the sandy shore of which rose heights, covered like the island with fine trees of varied foliage, while a glittering cascade falling from above formed a bright stream which made its way into the bay.

Having brought up as agreed on, we fired a gun, and Uncle Jack pulled off in the whale boat to pilot in the "Iris," which had hove to outside. In a short time we had the satisfaction of seeing her rounding the point, and she brought up near us. As she by this time had almost exhausted her stock of water, her boats and ours went in to obtain a supply. Hitherto no natives had been seen, but in case any should make their appearance, we had a guard with loaded muskets ready to protect the watering party. It occurred to us that had there been any natives in the neighbourhood the sound of our gun, which reverberated loudly among the hills, might have kept them at a distance. The operation of watering occupied us for the greater part of the day, and it was agreed that it was too late to set off in the boats until the following morning. In the meantime every preparation was made for the proposed expedition.

The chart, which was very imperfect, helped us but little, but by Captain Bingley's calculations the wreck was about twenty miles to the southward, which might take us, should the weather continue favourable, five or six hours to reach. We were to go on shore at the most convenient landing-place we could find to the northward of the spot, and try and open up a communication with any of the natives we might see, not knowing whether they might prove utter savages or semi-civilised, like the Malay tribes inhabiting many of the islands in the neighbourhood. We were to carry goods of various descriptions, axes and knives and coloured cloth, as well as beads and rings and looking-glasses.

I scarcely slept a wink during my watch below, thinking of the possibility of meeting with my father before the next day was over. I was to accompany Uncle Jack in the whale boat, in which as usual Ned and Bell were to pull. Our jolly-boat, under the charge of the boatswain, with Blyth, was also to come, and Captain Bingley agreed to accompany us in his long boat with a well-armed crew of six hands. We should thus muster pretty strong, and we might hope should the natives not prove friendly to keep them in awe. At daylight the following morning we started on our expedition. As there was a light breeze in our favour we were able to make sail, and to run down the coast, keeping within half a mile of the shore. It was generally rock-bound, but here and there were sandy bays, beyond which appeared a dense vegetation, a number of lofty trees rising above the brushwood. Sometimes we caught sight of bright streams making their way to the ocean, showing that the land was well watered. In the distance rose hills, many of considerable elevation, covered with trees almost to their summits. Altogether the country had a most attractive appearance. We wished that it could become the abode of civilised people, instead of the debased savages who were now said to inhabit it. After we had stood on for about twenty miles we began eagerly to look out for the wreck, but dark rocks alone met our view, some at a considerable distance from the land, others apparently joined to it.

"I fear that Captain Bingley must, after all, have been mistaken, for I see no signs of the wreck," I observed.

"We will stand on to the southward, however; he may easily have been deceived as to distance," answered Uncle Jack.

We had run on another mile or more when, looking back, I saw an object which seemed to me like the shattered hull of a ship. It had been previously hidden by the rocks along which we were coasting, and in a few minutes it would again have been concealed by a high ledge.

"Can that be the wreck?" I exclaimed, pointing it ought to Uncle Jack.

"No doubt about it," he answered, and he hailed Captain Bingley and Crowfoot.

We lowered our sails, and held a consultation as to how we could best approach the wreck, for such all hands agreed that it was. Uncle Jack accounted for the probability of its not having been seen by passing prahus, by its being concealed by the ledge, although visible over it from the mast-head of a ship. As there appeared to be an opening between the northern and southern ledges with clear water, Uncle Jack proposed to pull in, while the other boats, should he discover a passage, might follow. This was agreed to, and we steered in for the opening, Ned standing up in the bows, with a boat-hook in his hand, to watch for any sunken rocks, and to shove off should we come suddenly upon one. We found the water deeper than we expected, which accounted for the ship being driven in thus far without striking, while the ledges outside afterwards protected her from the seas which, during south-westerly gales, must have beaten on the coast. We found, however, that we could not get nearer.

"That's her; I have no doubt about it," exclaimed Ned, as we came full in sight of the wreck.

"I believe he is right," said Uncle Jack, as he surveyed the remains of the ship—"she is, I should judge, about the size of the 'Amphion.'"

We first tried to pull up towards her on the western side, but it being low water, so many rocks over which the boat could not pass intervening, we attempted to get round the south-eastern end of the ledge on which she lay, in the hope of finding deep water inside, between her and the land. In this we were not disappointed, and we found that there was a channel, an eighth of a mile wide, of deep water running between her and the beach. On ascertaining this, we pulled back near enough to the entrance, and made a signal for the other boats to come in. The whale boat again leading, we rounded the point and were not disappointed in finding that we could get sufficiently near the wreck to enable us, by scrambling over some rocks, to climb on board. Her masts were gone, the greater part of her upper works had been torn away, and I should not myself have recognised her as the once trim ship my father had commanded. Ned, however, who visited the forecastle, declared positively that she was the "Amphion," pointing out several marks on the bunks and the heel of the bowsprit.

W. H. G. Kingston

She had been completely gutted, not an article remaining in her, while attempts had been made apparently to set her on fire. This made us conjecture that she had been visited by Malay pirates, or perhaps by the Papuans from the neighbouring shore, though we saw no canoes by which they might have crossed over. The important point was thus settled, we had found the wreck of the "Amphion." We had next to ascertain if any of the crew survived.

We could see, however, no natives nor habitations of any sort. This might be accounted for from the fact that, for some distance inside the rocks the country was destitute of streams, and that the vegetation was much less luxuriant than in other parts we had before passed. We had now to determine whether to go further south, or to pull back and land as we had before intended, at the first place where native or other huts could be seen. As we had met with few habitations to the north, and had the greater part of the day before us, it was finally settled to sail further south. From Ned's account he had, after being cast on shore, been carried in that direction. We got out by the way we had come in, and then again making sail glided on for six or seven miles, when we came off the mouth of a river. Ned at once recognised the place, and said that he remembered a village a short way from the entrance. Accordingly, lowering our sails we pulled towards it. As the water was smooth, we had no difficulty in entering the river. Mangrove trees lined the shores on either side, but after pulling for about a mile, we came to openings, when trees of various sorts appeared. Shortly afterwards we saw on the right bank a number of huts, perched, like those of Borneo, on the tops of high poles, with ladders leading up to them. These, however, stood not on the shore, but on a level bank actually in the water. They were connected with each other by long bridges. The roofs were shaped like boats, bottom upwards. The poles were very irregular, some being twisted, others forked, while the buildings themselves had a dilapidated appearance. The walls were composed, as far as we could judge, of large mats, which, from the way they were secured, must have allowed a free circulation of air. Under the eaves of many of the houses we saw hung up several human skulls, which we supposed were those of enemies killed in war, but were, we afterwards found, the craniums of deceased relatives. Access to the shore from the village was obtained by a single wooden bridge. Hitherto we had seen no inhabitants, though we had no doubt some must have been in their houses, for we observed three or four canoes made fast to the posts below. Not to alarm them, we landed at a little distance where the depth of water enabled us to approach the bank, and taking ashore several of the articles we had brought for bartering, placed some before us, and held others up in our hands. As we kept our weapons concealed, our proceedings had the desired effect. In a few minutes a man's face with a huge mop-like head of frizzly hair appeared from behind one of the mats, then another and another. The first made his way along the bridge leading to the bank, stopping every now and then as if he doubted his own discretion in thus approaching us. Our friendly signs encouraged him, and he came on with less hesitation, followed by women of all ages, who now came out of the huts. The men were fine-looking fellows, their heads frizzled out in the most extraordinary manner. Most of them wore in their belts a knife and axe, besides smaller knives and a skin pouch, with a bamboo case containing betel root, tobacco, and lime. Most of the women were very unattractive, their dress consisting of strips of palm leaves worn tightly round the body, reaching to the knees and very dirty. The men were employed while watching us in "forking out"—for I cannot call it combing—their heads of hair with large wooden forks having four or five prongs. They wore earrings and necklaces made of white beads or kangaroo teeth. The earrings consisted of thick silver-wire hoops, some of the women having the ends of their necklaces attached to them, and then looped up into a sort of "chignon" behind. The men wore a great number of ornaments composed of the teeth of small animals, and they had finger rings as well as necklaces and bracelets. Some wore bands round their arms, ornamented with bunches of varied-coloured feathers. Others also had on anklets in the form of hoops made of shell, or brass wire, below the knee.

Ned and Charley were now told to try if they could make themselves understood, and to say that we had come as friends to trade with them and to give them all sorts of articles in exchange for the productions of their country, and then to inquire whether they had no white men among them. First Ned addressed them, then Charley. It was pretty evident, however, that the Papuans did not understand a word that was said. We therefore tried what signs would do, and succeded much better. Having come up to us, they examined the articles we had placed on the ground, when the chief man among them sent back several of the others to the village, who returned laden with mats and baskets, some empty, others full of a white flour, which on examination we found to be sago.

Also baskets of yams, taro, bananas, and other roots, cocoa-nuts, fruits, and oranges. We saw, indeed, a large number of cocoa-nut trees growing in the neighbourhood. We now offered them such of the goods as we had brought as we considered equivalent to the various lots.

Our trading had hitherto gone on well, and we hoped soon thoroughly to gain the confidence of the natives, and be able to make the inquiries we desired.

Kalong had come with us, and as he could not understand us, we told Ned to get him to try what he could do.

We watched him eagerly. After a time the Papuans appeared to understand what he was saying, they replied. He then turned and repeated what they had said to Ned, who told us that the Papuans acknowledged that some white men had been living with them for some time, but that they had been carried off by another tribe, who had come far away from the northward, at some distance from the coast. Before this they had made several attempts to escape, and were building a canoe for the purpose, when the enemy came down and made them prisoners.

Kalong was then directed to inquire what sort of people they were. I listened eagerly for Ned's interpretation; at last he said—

"One was a chief, who notwithstanding worked as willingly, or more so, than any of the rest, and seemed more anxious than they were to get away."

This description made me hope that it was my father of whom the Papuan spoke, but I was bitterly disappointed to hear that he had been carried to a distance, as it might still be long before we could find him. Uncle Jack felt as I did.

"We must, notwithstanding, keep up our spirits, Harry," he said; "there's no proof that he has lost his life, and as these savages don't move far from their locations, we may soon have a chance of communicating with him. We must try and get our friends here to help us, and the promise of a large reward may incite their wits and courage. Having succeeded thus far we will not give up the search, and if we can get one of these frizzly-pated gentlemen to act as our guide we will set off at once to look for him."

Uncle Jack explained his plans to Captain Bingley.

"I should like to make every effort in my power to recover my friend Musgrave, but I dare not risk the loss of any of my people in making the attempt," he answered.

"Then with your leave, Captain Bingley, I will go alone!" exclaimed Uncle Jack. "Who will volunteer? Ned, I am sure that you will be ready to go and look after your old captain."

"Aye, aye, sir," was the answer, "with all my heart."

"And I'll go too," said Bell, who had an eye to trade, and an idea that he might establish an intercourse with the natives, as he had done in Borneo.

Kalong, on being asked, expressed his readiness, provided that we all went well-armed.

"I'll join you," said Blyth; "I am sure Captain Haiselden will not object."

The next point to be arranged was, in the event of our finding my father, where should we rejoin the brig.

Captain Bingley, after some discussion, promised, concluding that Captain Haiselden would agree with him, to run down the coast, and to stand off and on, so as to be ready to take us on board. The appearance of the two vessels would, he hoped, produce a favourable effect on the natives. Uncle Jack thanked him heartily, and agreed that the plan was the best that could be devised. I had hoped that Captain Bingley, on hearing of the possibility of my father being in the neighbourhood, would have marched with our whole force to rescue him, but he observed that so large a party might make the natives suspect that we had come as enemies, whereas a small force would show that we had no hostile intentions, and induce them to behave in a friendly manner towards us.

Blyth now told Ned to inform the natives, through Kalong, that we should be ready to purchase all the sago they could obtain, as well as a small quantity of cocoa-nuts, yams, and other roots or fruits, promising to call for them before we left the coast. The natives, who seemed fully to enter into the spirit of trade, were highly satisfied, and undertook to do as they were advised.

Blyth said that if we could open up a trade with them it might lead to a commercial intercourse with other tribes along the coast, and ultimately, he hoped, to the civilisation of the country; observing, "If we can show the natives that we wish to be friendly, and treat them with justice, we shall render them service while we benefit ourselves."

As Captain Bingley was anxious to get back before nightfall, his and the boatswain's boats started on their return, leaving Uncle Jack, Blyth, and me with the three men to carry out our proposed undertaking.

W. H. G. Kingston

CHAPTER SEVEN

We felt pretty well satisfied of the friendly intentions of the natives, but Uncle Jack considered that it would be prudent to be on our guard, and directed us all to keep close together. We feared, from the long discussion held by the natives, that we should find a difficulty in obtaining guides, none of them being willing to encounter the dangers they expected to meet with. We told Kalong to offer a handsome payment to each man who would accompany us, and at length two fine young fellows stepped forward and agreed to go. They would not, however, consent to start until the following morning at daybreak. They offered one of their huts that we might rest in it at night. We selected one which overhung the stream, so that we might secure our boat beneath and retreat to it if necessary. The inhabitants of the hut, who had no heavy articles of furniture to remove, at once cleared out and gave us possession.

As evening approached we saw them cooking in large earthen bowls. Supper consisted of yams, vegetables, fish, and pork, some dishes being seasoned with cocoa-nut, finely shred over them, and all very well cooked. This showed us that the natives were not the savages they have so generally been represented to be, and the hospitable treatment we received gave us confidence that they intended to act honestly.

Night passed away quietly, and the next morning, after a further supply of cooked provisions had been brought us, our two guides said that they were ready to start. They told Kalong that they intended to row along the coast some distance to the eastward, where there was a bay in which we could land, and from thence proceed directly towards a village perched on the side of a mountain, where the white men had been living when last heard of.

We agreed at once to embark. Pulling down the river, for there was no wind for sailing, we steered as the natives directed. The shore, as far as we could see, was densely wooded, with high hills, also covered with trees, rising in the far distance into lofty mountain ranges. Here and there were openings in the forest through which we could distinguish villages, but the natives either did not see us, or supposed that the whale boat was one of their own canoes.

At all events we were not followed. We had rowed fifteen and twenty miles when our pilots pointed to an opening on the shore, off which we had arrived. A short distance ahead we saw lying off the coast a small island thickly covered with trees. Eager to land, scarcely giving it a second glance, we pulled in for the bay the natives pointed out. As we approached we observed near the beach a number of houses similar to those of our friends, and fully expected to encounter fresh difficulties with the natives, but on getting nearer we saw no one moving about.

We told Kalong to ask whether the people were likely to prove friendly or not. After consulting with our guides he answered that the huts were deserted, the whole of the inhabitants having been carried off by a fleet of prahus which lately visited the coast.

On landing we found that this account was correct. Looking

out for some thick underwood we dragged up our whale boat on the beach, and so concealed her that she could not be seen by strangers entering the bay. We now prepared for our march. We each of us carried, besides our arms and ammunition, some biscuits, tea, and sugar, a small bale of goods consisting of coloured cloth, axes, knives, beads, and glittering ornaments likely to suit the savage taste.

Ned and Charley had, besides, our simple cooking utensils. We felt sure of obtaining game enough and wild fruits to enable us to fare sumptuously.

Blyth and I were in high spirits, for I felt sure ere long that we should find my father, and I was surprised that Uncle Jack did not appear equally confident. We found the woods as we proceeded full of birds of magnificent plumage, parrots, cockatoos, lories, and others of exquisite form and colour, which Blyth at once declared were birds of paradise. They, however, kept at such a distance that we were unable to shoot any of them had we been so disposed. Looking up at the top of a lofty tree we saw a large number flying backwards and forwards from branch to branch, so that the trees appeared filled with waving plumes. We stopped for a moment to admire them. Their wings were raised directly over their backs. Their heads were stretched out, while their long hinder feathers, being elevated and expanded, formed two superb fans. The heads of the birds were yellow, their throats emerald green, but we could scarcely distinguish the tints amid the rich golden glory which waved above them. Magnificent butterflies, also of the most gorgeous colours, flew round us, and glittering beetles, of equally beautiful tints, crept along the ground or up the stems of the trees. In one or two open spots we startled several kangaroos of a small species which went hopping away, looking back curiously at us every now and then. Suddenly also we came upon a cassowary, a wingless bird, the body of which is about twice the size of a large turkey, but its long legs raise it to the height of five or six feet from the ground. It is covered with long close black hair like feathers. The skin of the neck is bare, and it is of a bright blue and red. Instead of wings it has on its sides a bunch of horny black spines like porcupine quills. There are several species which differ in appearance from each other.

Mr Blyth told me there must be at least eighteen species of birds of paradise, inhabiting different localities. The commonest is yellow with a long tail of the same colour. We saw numerous pigeons also, and a curious animal called the cuscus, something like an opossum, with a long tail, small head, large eyes, and a dense covering of woolly fur. We observed traces also of other animals, but what they were we could not make out—perhaps some large species of kangaroo or deer. I mention these creatures together to show the abundance of animal life in Papua. But, as may be supposed, we had no time to attend to natural history, our great object being, as soon as possible, to meet the tribe among whom our countrymen were said to be living. We travelled on until night approached, when our guides signified that we must form a camp. They set to work by first clearing away the grass and examining the neighbouring bushes to be satisfied that neither snakes nor savage animals lurked within. They then told Kalong to cut a quantity of bamboos which grew on the banks of a stream a short distance off. With these they quickly formed a hut, to which they fixed a floor at some distance from the ground to serve as a sleeping-place. It was thatched with large leaves, and was of sufficient size to hold all the party when somewhat closely packed. Uncle Jack, Blyth, and I kept watch by turns, though our guides did not seem to consider this necessary. We were not disturbed with the various sounds which came out of the forest, produced, however, I believe, rather by insects and birds than by wild beasts.

W. H. G. Kingston

Next morning, after cooking several birds which we had shot and taken our breakfast, we recommenced our journey. We had marched on five or six miles up a gradual ascent, differing, however, very little from the ground we had left, when our guides informed us that we were approaching the village for which we were bound. Soon after we saw in the distance a large number of leaf-covered huts stretching over a considerable extent of ground. It was agreed that our guides should go forward, each provided with some of the articles we had brought to present to the chief, and to say that some white strangers had arrived who desired to become friends and to trade with him. We told Kalong that they must not fail to hint that we were well-armed and able to defend ourselves, but at the same time that we were peaceably disposed. Observing a rock a short distance off, partly covered with trees, from which we could command a view of the country around us, we climbed to the top of it to wait there in the shade until the return of the two Papuans. We employed part of the time in making a meal off the provisions which we had cooked in the morning. How eagerly I looked out for our guides, expecting to see them perhaps accompanied by my father. We waited and waited, but still nowhere could we discover them. At length, a large portion of the day having passed, we saw a person hurrying towards us, and as he began to climb the rock we perceived that he was one of our Papuan friends. His countenance showed that he was greatly agitated. We anxiously waited until Kalong and Ned could interpret for us.

"He brings bad news, sir," said Ned, at length; "from what I can make out, the savages have seized his companion, and he had a hard job to get away from them. He says that some of the white men are dead, and that the others, not long ago, made their escape. This made the people very savage, and he fears if we go near them that they will seize and keep us instead."

"But, my father! Do you make out that he has escaped?" I inquired eagerly.

"It is a very difficult question to answer," said Ned; "our friend here thinks that the man whom they call the 'White Chief,' and who I take it was the captain, did get away, and that makes them so angry. It seems that they had been very friendly with him up to that time, only they would not let him go because he was teaching them all sorts of things. I don't suppose if they were to make us prisoners they would kill us, but we should lose our object in coming, and may be they would keep too strict a watch to let us escape."

We had no reason to doubt our guide; indeed, his story appeared so probable that Uncle Jack at once resolved to beat a retreat. If the white men had escaped, they were now probably on the coast, and we might fall in with them.

This hope greatly softened the disappointment we should otherwise have felt. Our native friend seemed satisfied with our resolution. We inquired what he intended to do with regard to his companion. He replied that he would not lose his life, and that he would probably some day make his escape, and when we told him that he should have the promised reward notwithstanding the failure of the expedition, he was evidently highly satisfied.

There was no time to be lost, as we wished to put as great a distance as possible between ourselves and the villagers before they discovered that we had begun to retreat. We had the advantage of knowing the way and of a beaten track to traverse. Our loads, too, were lightened somewhat by the presents we had sent; at the same time Uncle Jack thought it would be imprudent to throw the remainder away, lest they should fall into the hands of our pursuers, who would consequently be less likely to come to terms with us, should

W. H. G. Kingston

we be overtaken. It was dark when we reached our camping-place. As our guide undertook to lead us back to our boat during the night, we continued our journey without waiting to rest. We could see the stars through the opening of the forest, and we knew that we were going in the right direction. Without our native guide, however, we could not have ventured to make the attempt. With due thankfulness we at length caught sight of the ocean, on which the light from a crescent moon was glittering brightly.

Our boat was safe, but it was a question whether we should launch her at once, or remain on shore until the following morning. As we were all pretty well tired, Uncle Jack determined on turning her bottom up, so that we might sleep beneath her while one of us kept watch in case any natives should approach. We dragged her out from among the bushes, therefore, down to the beach, just above high water mark, so that we might be able to put off quickly should it become necessary. Of course we could think and talk only of one subject. What had become of my father?

We must of course continue our search for him, and we all hoped that, unless he had escaped on board some passing vessel, which was not at all likely, he would not be far off.

It was arranged that Blyth should keep the first watch, Uncle Jack the second, and I the third.

I never slept more soundly in my life, as I was very tired with our long tramp, for it seemed but a moment after I lay down before I was aroused by my uncle giving me a pull by the leg I crept out from under the boat, and shouldering my musket began to pace up and down close to the boat to keep myself awake, while my uncle took my place.

The stars were shining brightly, and a light wind rustled the leaves of the neighbouring trees, while the water lapped gently on the beach. No other sounds reached my ears. I still felt so drowsy that I was sure, should I sit down, that I should go to sleep. Occasionally I extended my walk to the borders of the forest.

I had made several turns, and calculated that I had been half an hour or so on watch, when it appeared to me that the night was growing darker, and looking up I saw that the stars overhead were obscured, while the murmuring sound in the trees had increased in loudness; though sheltered as we were by the forest we did not feel the wind, which was blowing off shore. The clouds continued gathering until the whole sky was obscured. I fully expected before long that there would be a downpour of rain, but as we were on a weather shore I did not think it necessary to call my companions. I continued my walk, occasionally approaching the forest and then returning to the boat.

I looked out anxiously for the approach of day, but even had the sky been clear, the trees would have prevented me from seeing the first streaks of dawn, and as it was the sun itself would probably not be visible.

At last I knew by the light that the day had broke. I had gone back to the forest, and intended to arouse my companions at the end of the next turn, when I fancied that I could distinguish the sound of human voices amid the soughing of the wind in the branches overhead. Stooping down to the ground I listened attentively—I was sure I was not mistaken.

The voices might be those of the natives, who finding we had retreated had pursued us. Hurrying back to the boat as quickly as I could, I roused up Uncle Jack, telling him what I had heard.

W. H. G. Kingston

"Very likely you are right, Harry," he answered, "though we might drive back the savages, we could not do so without bloodshed, and our safest plan will be to get our boat off and hold a parley with them from her. If they show hostility, we can keep them at bay until we get to a safe distance."

Without a moment's delay we called up our companions. We quickly turned the boat on her keel and ran her down into the water. We two held her, while the rest carried our goods on board.

Just as we were jumping in we saw a number of savages, armed with spears and bows, emerging from the forest, and they, catching sight of us, rushed forward, others following, until a formidable band was collected on the beach.

"Shove off, lads!" cried the first mate, seizing an oar, and the rest of us imitating his example, aided by the wind, we speedily drove the boat away from the shore.

The savages, seeing us about to escape them, bent their bows and let fly a shower of arrows, which came whistling about our ears, some falling in the boat and others on either side.

The first mate steered, Blyth sat by his side with a musket in his hand ready to fire, while our Papuan guide crouched down in the stern-sheets.

"Shall I fire?" asked Blyth, "I can knock over one of those fellows; the chief, I suspect, who seems to be leading them on."

"No, hold fast, I would not injure the poor wretches if it can be avoided," answered the first mate. "We shall be out of their reach in another minute. We can then settle how to treat with them."

A few strokes took us beyond the range of their missiles. He was right, for their bows were comparatively small, intended rather to shoot birds than for war, while their javelins could not be thrown to any great distance.

He now directed Ned to tell Kalong to address them, and to say that we had come with friendly intentions to trade, and to recover some countrymen who had been wrecked on their coast.

The chief, on hearing this, invited us on shore, observing that we could talk more easily there, and that he would hear what we had to say.

The Malay and our native guide talked together.

"Kalong says we had better not trust them," observed Ned; "if we land they may shoot us for the sake of getting our goods. They don't know how far our firearms can reach. Better give them a volley to show them."

This Uncle Jack was unwilling to do, though we might have shot down half a dozen of them at least, had we fired as Ned proposed.

While this palaver was going forward I took a glance seaward, when what was my astonishment to see the "Iris" and "Lily" standing along the coast, under close reefed topsails, as if coming to look for us. I could judge by the way they heeled over that a pretty strong breeze was blowing in the offing.

If we were to get on board there was no time to lose; indeed, it seemed very doubtful whether we could reach either of the vessels. They were too far off to see us, and it was doubtful whether they could hear our muskets. Uncle Jack directed

Blyth and me to fire at the same time, but neither the ship nor the brig altered their course. They had good reason for not wishing to approach the land, as the wind, rapidly increasing, was shifting to the north-west, and they might at any moment find themselves on a lee shore. They had also got so far from the harbour they had left that it was evident that they could not manage to get back.

"They'll not desert us, lads, depend upon that," said Uncle Jack, as we saw them standing away from the coast; "we can neither overtake them nor land while those fellows on shore show so unfriendly a disposition. We must try and get back to the village where we procured our guides, though I don't know what sort of reception we shall meet with when their friends hear that we have lost one of them. It will be a long pull and a heavy one, for we shall have a head sea as soon as we get clear of this bay."

"Why not then make for yonder island to the eastward?" I observed. "These savages, who don't appear to have any canoes, cannot follow us there, and we shall be able to remain in safety until our friends come to take us off."

"We may have to follow your suggestion, Harry, but we must first try to get back to the river to land our guide according to our promise. He has proved faithful, and we will supply him with goods with which he may be able to ransom his companion."

This was said as we were pulling out of the bay, but no sooner did we get beyond the point than we met so heavy a sea that it was impossible to pull the whale boat against it, and we were in danger of being swamped. Our only alternative was, as I proposed, to run for the island. Even now we had to pull hard to avoid the following seas which threatened to poop us. We saw the savages on shore dancing, shouting, and gesticulating when they discovered that we had escaped them. On finding, however, that we were steering for the island they rushed along the beach in the same direction, which made us fear that they might possess the means of crossing over to it, and that after all we should have to fight for our lives. We had not much apprehension, however, as to the result. Uncle Jack intended to pull round to the lee side of the island, and then, should they persist in attacking us, we could shoot them down from the boat while we kept out of range of their arrows.

As we pulled along we watched the two vessels which were getting further and further from the coast, although the ship had only her fore and mizen topsail set, and the brig was under equally snug canvas.

Aided by the wind the boat went faster than the savages could run, and they were out of sight when we reached the passage between the island and the main land. We could see no canoes on the shore, and this made us hope that we might at all events avoid an attack until the gale was over, and we could resume our search for my father.

We did not doubt for a moment that the "Lily" would come to look for us, and by hoisting a signal on the outer end of the island we hoped to attract her attention. Passing through the channel, which was about a mile wide, we rounded the eastern point of the island where the water was perfectly smooth, when discovering a small bay with a sandy beach we at once pulled in. As we saw no huts or plantations we calculated that the island was uninhabited. We therefore landed without hesitation, and hauled up our boat. From a rocky elevation on the northern side of the bay we could command a view of the main land along the whole length of the strait.

W. H. G. Kingston

Uncle Jack sent Blyth and me to watch should any natives appear, but sharp as were our eyes we could discover neither canoes nor human beings moving about.

The savages therefore supposing we had escaped had, we concluded, returned to their village. As there was some probability that we should have to remain several days on the island, Uncle Jack proposed that we should build a hut, which would be a pleasanter sleeping-place than under the boat. We at once therefore set to work.

The Papuan showed himself an adept at the use of the axe, and understanding clearly what we wanted was of great assistance. A bamboo thicket and some large palm leaves afforded us materials, so that in a short time we had a well built hut erected capable of containing all the party, the upper floor affording us a sleeping-place, while the lower would shelter us during the day should it come on to rain. We naturally felt much anxiety about the vessels, though we trusted that they would avoid any of the dangers which lay to the westward.

Night passed without any adventure. The gale raged with unabated fury, though we felt it but little in our sheltered cove. We had brought a good store of provisions and a breaker of water in the boat, but that, from the frequent applications to it, was almost exhausted. It was necessary to search for a fresh supply. Uncle Jack was unwilling to leave the beach in case the natives might find the means of crossing. Blyth and I therefore undertook to go in search of water. We hoped, although we might not discover a stream— which from the size of the island was unlikely—we might find a spring, or ground by digging into which fresh water might be reached. As soon, therefore, as we had breakfasted we set off. As we had pulled along it the previous day we calculated that the island was between three and four miles long and about two miles broad.

Besides our guns we each carried a long bamboo stick, one end pointed and the other formed like a gouge to serve as a spade, with which we might dig for water, should we fail to find a stream.

So thick was the jungle immediately at the back of the cove that we had to proceed along the shore some distance before we could make our way inland. In several places we found it lined with the pandanus or screw palm, which looks as if it had branches at both ends, the lower being the roots which had lifted the trunk into the air. In other places there were cocoa-nut trees with nuts hanging from them, so we knew that even were we to be kept there many weeks we should have an ample supply of vegetable diet.

"We shall find other food too," said Blyth, pointing to some trees which grew in a hollow at the foot of a hill. "Those are sago trees; if hard pressed we might manufacture sufficient sago from them to last us for months, or even years. They require moisture, and I have little doubt that by digging we shall find water not far from their roots. But we will search further, perhaps we may discover a spring which will give us a more ample supply, so that there is no fear of our starving. What a number of birds there are! Many of them, too are birds of paradise. I cannot tell you their names, but they seem to be the same as are found in the Aru islands away to the southward. We shall have no difficulty in shooting them, or some of those magnificent pigeons when we want them, but it would be a pity to expend our ammunition unnecessarily. We can kill a few as we return to serve us for dinner."

The whole of the island indeed appeared to be a perfect garden, and yet, as far as we could discover, not a single

W. H. G. Kingston

inhabitant did it contain. We made our way on, not without great difficulty, sometimes having to cut a passage for ourselves through the underwood until we reached the southern end, or rather western shore, where we could see the ocean still covered over with raging foam-topped seas, which made us fear that for many days to come our friends could not return, and until the brig did come back I was sure that Uncle Jack would consider it his duty to remain on the island, whence he could communicate with her.

As we were more likely to find a spring inland than on the coast we continued our course up the centre of the island. "We shall have to dig, I suspect, after all, in the sago grove," said Blyth, as we at last began our return. "However, we may as well carry some game with us; I intend to shoot the first fine pigeon I see. You can try your luck, although I would advise you not to fire unless you feel sure of your aim."

In a short time Blyth, who was a good shot, killed three or four pigeons, and I had shot a parrot and a bird of paradise, but I felt ashamed at having deprived so beautiful a creature of life, yet thousands were flying about unseen by human eye, which they are formed to delight. We went on a little further, when I again fired and brought down another parrot. Just as I pulled the trigger I caught sight between the trees of a face watching us. At the first glance I thought it must be some huge baboon, but still it looked human though covered thickly with hair. I was a little in advance of Blyth. Supposing that if not a baboon it was a savage, I was hurriedly reloading, ready to defend myself, when a man stepping forward exclaimed—

"Who are you mates, and where do you come from?"

For a moment my astonishment at the sudden apparition prevented me from answering. The man, however, advanced without fear. His dress, though in tatters, was that of a seaman, fastened together by all sorts of contrivance, while a roughly-formed palm-leaf hat covered his head.

"I heard your shots some time ago, and have been long hunting for you, for I was sure no natives could have fired as you have done."

Without answering his inquiries, I with intense eagerness put the same questions, "Who are you? And where do you come from?"

"I am an Englishman, who was cast away out there, and who was kept a prisoner for many a long year by a set of savages up the country, until about six months ago, when the captain and I got free from them and crossed over here, where we have been ever since, hoping that some craft would appear and take us off."

"What ship did you belong to? Who is your captain?" I asked, with intense eagerness.

"The 'Amphion,' Captain Musgrave was my captain," he answered.

"He is not, then, living?"

"Yes, he is alive, but he is in a bad way, I fear. He kept up his spirits until yesterday, when we saw two English vessels run past us to the southward. Then it seemed to him, and to me too, for that matter, that all hope was gone, and that we might have to remain here for years more for what we could tell, since all the time we have been here we have never seen a vessel."

At that moment Blyth came up, and in a voice choking with

agitation I told him what I had heard.

"Lead us at once to your captain," he said, turning to the seaman; "we came here expressly to look for him, and are expecting the vessels back as soon as the weather will allow them to return to the coast. If your father is ill, Harry, there will be a risk in agitating him by presenting yourself suddenly to him. Let our friend here first tell him that he has found some Englishmen on the island, and then I will go in and tell him that his son and brother-in-law have come to look for him. Where is he living?" he asked of the sailor.

"In a poor enough place, sir, close on the sea shore. It is a cave, inside a rock. We thought it safer than a hut, where the natives, if they had come to the island, would be more likely to find us."

I begged the seaman to hurry on. "What! Are you the captain's son?" he asked, as I ran by his side. "Often and often he has talked about you. If anything will set him on his legs the sight of you will."

We soon reached the beach, when scrambling for some distance among the rocks the seaman pointed to the entrance of a cave at the side of a hill which sloped up from the water.

As agreed on the seaman went first, followed by Blyth. I stood outside eagerly waiting to be summoned. It seemed so long that I was afraid my father had been overcome with the news.

At length Blyth appeared, and beckoned me in, and the next instant I was kneeling by my father's side, as he lay stretched on a bed of leaves and matting, which Dick Meade, his faithful follower, had arranged for him.

"What! Are you Harry, really my son Harry?" he exclaimed, throwing his arms around my neck; "I was sure that you and my good brother Jack Radburn would come to look for me if you thought I was alive, and not until yesterday, when God in his mercy had sent you to this island, did I lose hope. Ungrateful I was, after having been preserved from so many dangers; but your appearance has brought me back to life."

"What the captain wants is some good food," I heard Dick observe to Blyth; "if you'll let me cook one of those pigeons it will do him all the good in the world."

As Blyth carried a flint and steel they soon had a fire lighted in a sheltered spot, just outside the cave. While I sat by my father I was thankful to see that he appeared stronger as we conversed.

Blyth soon again came in and volunteered to carry the joyful intelligence to Uncle Jack. During his absence the pigeon was cooked and eaten. Dick brought in a shell full of water from a spring, which he said bubbled out of the hill side close at hand.

Soon I heard Uncle Jack's voice. I need not describe the meeting between him and my father. He had left Blyth with directions to bring the boat round should the sea have gone down sufficiently to enable her without risk to reach a little cove which we found not far from the cave, where she might be hauled up if necessary. Uncle Jack, with his usual forethought, had brought tea and sugar and biscuit, luxuries to which my poor father had long been a stranger. They appeared to benefit him much. In a few hours he was able to sit up and converse freely with us. Before nightfall we had the satisfaction of seeing the boat, and Dick ran down to pilot her into the cove. Some of the party spent the night in the cave, which was of considerable size, and others under the boat.

The first thing all hands did in the morning was to cut down the tallest trees we could find to form a flag-staff, which we placed on the highest part of the hill overlooking the ocean. We then fastened together the two flags we had in the boat with a number of our handkerchiefs, which, combined, formed a flag of a size which could be seen at a considerable distance; eagerly we watched day after day for the appearance of sail.

I had never seen Uncle Jack so anxious, he could not help reflecting that during the gale some accident might have happened to the "Iris," and that his dear Grace might be among the sufferers.

"Cheer up, brother Jack," said my father, when he saw him thus cast down; "I have learned more than ever to put confidence in God's loving mercy during my exile. Had I not been able to trust Him, I should have sank long ago. I have known Haiselden and Bingley all their lives, and they are not the men to desert their friends."

Still another and another day passed. At length, one morning, I was awakened by a shout from Dick Meade, and running out of the cave, I saw the rising sun shining on the white canvas of a brig in the offing. That she was the "Lily" I had no doubt, but where was the "Iris"? What would be Uncle Jack's feelings at not seeing her?

Dick was hoisting up the flag which he had just bent on. The breeze was from the south-east, which would enable the brig to approach the island without risk. She was standing on farther to the northward, and I began to fear that she was not the "Lily" after all. I was expressing my doubts to Dick, when I found Uncle Jack standing by me with a telescope to his eye.

"Yes she's the 'Lily,' no doubt about it; she'll see our signal before long, as she will be looking out for us."

In another minute the whole of our party were on foot. I ran in to tell my father, who insisted on coming out to have a look at the object for which his eyes had so often ached in vain.

In the meantime our men had lighted a fire, believing that a long pull would be before them. Fortunate it was that they did so. My father was not in a fit state to go off without breakfast. The meal was scarcely over when the brig tacked, and the "Lily's" flag was run up at the mast-head.

Not a moment was lost in launching the boat. My father was assisted down to the beach. We waited a few minutes, when the "Lily" hove to. Our last act was to lower the signal flag, and we then, getting on board, with hearty strokes pulled away for the brig.

"We have found him, we have found him!" I could not help calling out as we approached her side.

My father was helped on board, and warmly welcomed by our kind-hearted captain. Uncle Jack's first inquiry was for the "Iris."

"She's all safe at the Aru islands, where I promised to rejoin her as soon as I had recovered you," answered Captain Haiselden; "and as she has received some damage in the gale, she is likely to be detained there several days."

The only person who looked unhappy was our Papuan guide; but he was reassured when the captain promised to land him at his own village, towards which we stood, as soon as the whale boat was dropped astern.

In a couple of hours we were off the mouth of the river, when we once more pulled off, with the same party which had before landed in the whale boat.

As we approached, a shout of joy arose from our companions. The cause was soon explained. One of the first persons we saw standing on the platform in front of the hut was the lost guide who had, we afterwards found, made his escape, while his captors were pursuing us.

The natives were delighted with the things we brought them, and we could have laden our boat up to the gunwale with the articles they offered in return.

Wishing our friends good-bye, and promising that we would as soon as possible pay them another visit, we pulled back to the brig.

In three days we reached the Aru islands, seldom visited by English vessels, and brought up before the chief town Dobbo, which is, however, only a collection of huts such as those described in Papua and Borneo, though of a more substantial character. The population of the islands are mostly Papuans, though people from various other parts of the Eastern seas have settled there. The islands are generally level, and thickly wooded, the forests containing amongst other birds two or three of the most beautiful species of birds of paradise.

The "Iris" was almost ready to sail, so that we remained there but a couple of days, when, threading our way among the coral reefs, we once more got into the open sea.

I should have been happy to give a further description of our voyage and our visit to Timor, where we anchored to obtain fresh provisions. We then shaped our course along the south coast of Java, and then, crossing the Indian Ocean, rounded the Cape of Good Hope; after which we had a remarkably fine passage home, and, strange to say, did not once lose sight of the "Iris."

Whether Uncle Jack had anything to do with this I can only guess. I know that he told me to keep a bright look-out for her whenever he was below, and report to him any change in her position. The "Iris" led the way up the Thames. Immediately she dropped her anchor, before going into dock, Uncle Jack and my father went on board and arranged a plan with Grace for breaking the news of his return to my mother; she and Mrs Bingley at once went on shore promising to act with due discretion. I have every reason to believe they carried out their duty well, for when I arrived at home a few hours after my father, I found my mother looking the picture of happiness, and almost as calm and composed as usual.

I have not entered into the trading particulars of the voyages of the two vessels, but both were considered highly satisfactory. It was the first of several I made on board the brig to the same region, the mate of the "Lily" being now her captain.

In the next voyage my Aunt Grace, now Uncle Jack's wife, accompanied him. He has since retired from the sea. I served with him as his second, and then his first mate for some years, until I got the command of a ship. I must acknowledge that I greatly owe my success to having followed the good example set me by my excellent uncle once The Mate of the "Lily."

W. H. G. Kingston

ABOUT THE AUTHOR

William Henry Giles Kingston (1814 - 1880), writer of tales for boys, born in London, but spent much of his youth in Oporto, where his father was a merchant.

His first book, The Circassian Chief, appeared in 1844. His first book for boys, Peter the Whaler, was published in 1851, and had such success that he retired from business and devoted himself entirely to the production of this kind of literature, in which his popularity was deservedly great; and during 30 years he wrote upwards of 130 tales, including The Three Midshipmen (1862), The Three Lieutenants (1874), The Three Commanders (1875), The Three Admirals (1877), Digby Heathcote, etc.

He also conducted various papers, including The Colonist, and Colonial Magazine and East India Review. He was also interested in emigration, volunteering, and various philanthropic schemes. For services in negotiating a commercial treaty with Portugal he received a Portuguese knighthood, and for his literary labours a Government pension.

Choose from Thousands of 1stWorldLibrary Classics By

A. M. Barnard
Ada Leverson
Adolphus William Ward
Aesop
Agatha Christie
Alexander Aaronsohn
Alexander Kielland
Alexandre Dumas
Alfred Gatty
Alfred Ollivant
Alice Duer Miller
Alice Turner Curtis
Alice Dunbar
Allen Chapman
Alleyne Ireland
Ambrose Bierce
Amelia E. Barr
Amory H. Bradford
Andrew Lang
Andrew McFarland Davis
Andy Adams
Angela Brazil
Anna Alice Chapin
Anna Sewell
Annie Besant
Annie Hamilton Donnell
Annie Payson Call
Annie Roe Carr
Annonaymous
Anton Chekhov
Archibald Lee Fletcher
Arnold Bennett
Arthur C. Benson
Arthur Conan Doyle
Arthur M. Winfield
Arthur Ransome
Arthur Schnitzler
Arthur Train
Atticus
B.H. Baden-Powell
B. M. Bower
B. C. Chatterjee
Baroness Emmuska Orczy
Baroness Orczy
Basil King
Bayard Taylor
Ben Macomber
Bertha Muzzy Bower
Bjornstjerne Bjornson

Booth Tarkington
Boyd Cable
Bram Stoker
C. Collodi
C. E. Orr
C. M. Ingleby
Carolyn Wells
Catherine Parr Traill
Charles A. Eastman
Charles Amory Beach
Charles Dickens
Charles Dudley Warner
Charles Farrar Browne
Charles Ives
Charles Kingsley
Charles Klein
Charles Hanson Towne
Charles Lathrop Pack
Charles Romyn Dake
Charles Whibley
Charles Willing Beale
Charlotte M. Braeme
Charlotte M. Yonge
Charlotte Perkins Stetson
Clair W. Hayes
Clarence Day Jr.
Clarence E. Mulford
Clemence Housman
Confucius
Coningsby Dawson
Cornelis DeWitt Wilcox
Cyril Burleigh
D. H. Lawrence
Daniel Defoe
David Garnett
Dinah Craik
Don Carlos Janes
Donald Keyhoe
Dorothy Kilner
Dougan Clark
Douglas Fairbanks
E. Nesbit
E. P. Roe
E. Phillips Oppenheim
E. S. Brooks
Earl Barnes
Edgar Rice Burroughs
Edith Van Dyne
Edith Wharton

Edward Everett Hale
Edward J. O'Biren
Edward S. Ellis
Edwin L. Arnold
Eleanor Atkins
Eleanor Hallowell Abbott
Eliot Gregory
Elizabeth Gaskell
Elizabeth McCracken
Elizabeth Von Arnim
Ellem Key
Emerson Hough
Emilie F. Carlen
Emily Bronte
Emily Dickinson
Enid Bagnold
Enilor Macartney Lane
Erasmus W. Jones
Ernie Howard Pie
Ethel May Dell
Ethel Turner
Ethel Watts Mumford
Eugene Sue
Eugenie Foa
Eugene Wood
Eustace Hale Ball
Evelyn Everett-green
Everard Cotes
F. H. Cheley
F. J. Cross
F. Marion Crawford
Fannie E. Newberry
Federick Austin Ogg
Ferdinand Ossendowski
Fergus Hume
Florence A. Kilpatrick
Fremont B. Deering
Francis Bacon
Francis Darwin
Frances Hodgson Burnett
Frances Parkinson Keyes
Frank Gee Patchin
Frank Harris
Frank Jewett Mather
Frank L. Packard
Frank V. Webster
Frederic Stewart Isham
Frederick Trevor Hill
Frederick Winslow Taylor

Friedrich Kerst
Friedrich Nietzsche
Fyodor Dostoyevsky
G.A. Henty
G.K. Chesterton
Gabrielle E. Jackson
Garrett P. Serviss
Gaston Leroux
George A. Warren
George Ade
Geroge Bernard Shaw
George Cary Eggleston
George Durston
George Ebers
George Eliot
George Gissing
George MacDonald
George Meredith
George Orwell
George Sylvester Viereck
George Tucker
George W. Cable
George Wharton James
Gertrude Atherton
Gordon Casserly
Grace E. King
Grace Gallatin
Grace Greenwood
Grant Allen
Guillermo A. Sherwell
Gulielma Zollinger
Gustav Flaubert
H. A. Cody
H. B. Irving
H.C. Bailey
H. G. Wells
H. H. Munro
H. Irving Hancock
H. R. Naylor
H. Rider Haggard
H. W. C. Davis
Haldeman Julius
Hall Caine
Hamilton Wright Mabie
Hans Christian Andersen
Harold Avery
Harold McGrath
Harriet Beecher Stowe
Harry Castlemon
Harry Coghill
Harry Houidini

Hayden Carruth
Helent Hunt Jackson
Helen Nicolay
Hendrik Conscience
Hendy David Thoreau
Henri Barbusse
Henrik Ibsen
Henry Adams
Henry Ford
Henry Frost
Henry James
Henry Jones Ford
Henry Seton Merriman
Henry W Longfellow
Herbert A. Giles
Herbert Carter
Herbert N. Casson
Herman Hesse
Hildegard G. Frey
Homer
Honore De Balzac
Horace B. Day
Horace Walpole
Horatio Alger Jr.
Howard Pyle
Howard R. Garis
Hugh Lofting
Hugh Walpole
Humphry Ward
Ian Maclaren
Inez Haynes Gillmore
Irving Bacheller
Isabel Cecilia Williams
Isabel Hornibrook
Israel Abrahams
Ivan Turgenev
J.G.Austin
J. Henri Fabre
J. M. Barrie
J. M. Walsh
J. Macdonald Oxley
J. R. Miller
J. S. Fletcher
J. S. Knowles
J. Storer Clouston
J. W. Duffield
Jack London
Jacob Abbott
James Allen
James Andrews
James Baldwin

James Branch Cabell
James DeMille
James Joyce
James Lane Allen
James Lane Allen
James Oliver Curwood
James Oppenheim
James Otis
James R. Driscoll
Jane Abbott
Jane Austen
Jane L. Stewart
Janet Aldridge
Jens Peter Jacobsen
Jerome K. Jerome
Jessie Graham Flower
John Buchan
John Burroughs
John Cournos
John F. Kennedy
John Gay
John Glasworthy
John Habberton
John Joy Bell
John Kendrick Bangs
John Milton
John Philip Sousa
John Taintor Foote
Jonas Lauritz Idemil Lie
Jonathan Swift
Joseph A. Altsheler
Joseph Carey
Joseph Conrad
Joseph E. Badger Jr
Joseph Hergesheimer
Joseph Jacobs
Jules Vernes
Julian Hawthrone
Julie A Lippmann
Justin Huntly McCarthy
Kakuzo Okakura
Karle Wilson Baker
Kate Chopin
Kenneth Grahame
Kenneth McGaffey
Kate Langley Bosher
Kate Langley Bosher
Katherine Cecil Thurston
Katherine Stokes
L. A. Abbot
L. T. Meade

L. Frank Baum
Latta Griswold
Laura Dent Crane
Laura Lee Hope
Laurence Housman
Lawrence Beasley
Leo Tolstoy
Leonid Andreyev
Lewis Carroll
Lewis Sperry Chafer
Lilian Bell
Lloyd Osbourne
Louis Hughes
Louis Joseph Vance
Louis Tracy
Louisa May Alcott
Lucy Fitch Perkins
Lucy Maud Montgomery
Luther Benson
Lydia Miller Middleton
Lyndon Orr
M. Corvus
M. H. Adams
Margaret E. Sangster
Margret Howth
Margaret Vandercook
Margaret W. Hungerford
Margret Penrose
Maria Edgeworth
Maria Thompson Daviess
Mariano Azuela
Marion Polk Angellotti
Mark Overton
Mark Twain
Mary Austin
Mary Catherine Crowley
Mary Cole
Mary Hastings Bradley
Mary Roberts Rinehart
Mary Rowlandson
M. Wollstonecraft Shelley
Maud Lindsay
Max Beerbohm
Myra Kelly
Nathaniel Hawthrone
Nicolo Machiavelli
O. F. Walton
Oscar Wilde

Owen Johnson
P.G. Wodehouse
Paul and Mabel Thorne
Paul G. Tomlinson
Paul Severing
Percy Brebner
Percy Keese Fitzhugh
Peter B. Kyne
Plato
Quincy Allen
R. Derby Holmes
R. L. Stevenson
R. S. Ball
Rabindranath Tagore
Rahul Alvares
Ralph Bonehill
Ralph Henry Barbour
Ralph Victor
Ralph Waldo Emmerson
Rene Descartes
Ray Cummings
Rex Beach
Rex E. Beach
Richard Harding Davis
Richard Jefferies
Richard Le Gallienne
Robert Barr
Robert Frost
Robert Gordon Anderson
Robert L. Drake
Robert Lansing
Robert Lynd
Robert Michael Ballantyne
Robert W. Chambers
Rosa Nouchette Carey
Rudyard Kipling
Saint Augustine
Samuel B. Allison
Samuel Hopkins Adams
Sarah Bernhardt
Sarah C. Hallowell
Selma Lagerlof
Sherwood Anderson
Sigmund Freud
Standish O'Grady
Stanley Weyman
Stella Benson
Stella M. Francis

Stephen Crane
Stewart Edward White
Stijn Streuvels
Swami Abhedananda
Swami Parmananda
T. S. Ackland
T. S. Arthur
The Princess Der Ling
Thomas A. Janvier
Thomas A Kempis
Thomas Anderton
Thomas Bailey Aldrich
Thomas Bulfinch
Thomas De Quincey
Thomas Dixon
Thomas H. Huxley
Thomas Hardy
Thomas More
Thornton W. Burgess
U. S. Grant
Upton Sinclair
Valentine Williams
Various Authors
Vaughan Kester
Victor Appleton
Victor G. Durham
Victoria Cross
Virginia Woolf
Wadsworth Camp
Walter Camp
Walter Scott
Washington Irving
Wilbur Lawton
Wilkie Collins
Willa Cather
Willard F. Baker
William Dean Howells
William le Queux
W. Makepeace Thackeray
William W. Walter
William Shakespeare
Winston Churchill
Yei Theodora Ozaki
Yogi Ramacharaka
Young E. Allison
Zane Grey